What Every 18-Year-Old Needs to Know about Texas Law

What Every 18-Year-Old Needs to Know about Texas Law

Revised Edition

L. Jean Wallace

 University of Texas Press, Austin

txr

Revised Edition, 1997

Requests for permission to reproduce material from this work should be sent to
Permissions, University of Texas Press, Box 7819, Austin, TX 78713-7819.

∞ The paper used in this publication meets the minimum requirements of American National Standard for Information Sciences—Permanence of Paper for Printed Library Materials, ANSI Z39.48–1984.

Library of Congress Cataloging-in-Publication Data

Wallace, L. Jean (Lily Jean), 1951–
    What every 18-year-old needs to know about Texas law / by L. Jean Wallace. —Rev. ed.
        p.   cm.
    Includes index.
    Summary: Presents general information on the broad range of basic rights, responsibilities, and penalties relating to Texas laws with true anecdotes inserted to illustrate the material.
    ISBN 0-292-79119-4 (pbk. : alk. paper)
    1. Law—Texas—Popular works. [1. Law—Texas.] I. Title.
KFT1281.W28   1997
349.764—dc21   96-54799

Dedicated to My Mother

Contents

Introduction

You're 18. You are now an adult under the laws of the State of Texas, for all purposes except the drinking of alcoholic beverages. With your new rights come responsibilities. Violation of these responsibilities can have serious penalties that never occurred to you at the time of the violation. The purpose of this book is to acquaint you with the broad range of basic rights, responsibilities, and penalties so that you may know before you act. This book will also set straight some common legal misconceptions. The information is general and intended for information purposes only. If you have a specific legal problem, you should always seek advice from an attorney. Remember, the laws discussed are for the State of Texas only. Laws in other states may be very different.

Special Note about the True Stories: Periodically, I have inserted in the text a true story to illustrate the material. These stories are absolutely true, but they did not all happen to one hapless family.

I heard them all in my capacity as attorney for students at Texas Tech University. In that position I was not allowed to represent students in court. I could only give advice. Sometimes it was hard to give the advice with a straight face.

Fortunately, most student problems were not tragic, but just painful lessons on the road to maturity. I hope I helped smooth that path for the students I counseled.

While I hope the stories amuse you, I also hope you won't miss the point.

What Every 18-Year-Old Needs to Know about Texas Law

Rules to Live By

1. Life is not fair.

2. Anything that sounds too good to be true usually is.

3. There is no such thing as a free lunch.

4. Ignorance of the law is no excuse.

5. Follow the Golden Rule: Do unto others as you would have them do unto you.

6. When in doubt, check it out.

Chapter 1
Cars and Motorcycles

Traffic Tickets

In case you've been so lucky as to have reached eighteen without receiving a traffic ticket, I'll begin with the basics.

1.1 *Pull Over When You See the Red Lights.* Even if you doubt that the officer means you, pull over. Few things make an officer madder than to have someone delay stopping. Usually the siren or loudspeaker is used only as a last resort. Don't wait. Pull over now. If the officer doesn't want you, he or she will go on past and no harm is done.

SPECIAL NOTE: To those of you who grew up watching certain TV shows and movies in which the civilian always outruns the officer—getting pulled over is REALITY, not TV. In real life, the officers are better drivers, there are more of them, and they always get you in the end.

True Story Number One

A motorcycle can always outrun a car, right? Not necessarily.

Meet Joe Anyone, who is riding his brand-new motorcycle on the city streets for the first time. He is so carried away with enjoyment, he neglects to make a complete stop at a stop sign. His enjoyment turns to horror when he glances back and sees a police car right behind him with the red lights on.

Panic city! His motorcycle is unregistered, uninspected, and uninsured, and he is unlicensed for a motorcycle. Without thinking, he accelerates and the chase is on.

Several blocks and numerous traffic violations later, Joe is headed for an intersection with a very busy street. Ignoring the stop sign would be suicidal. He attempts a quick stop. Alas, the intersection was newly graveled. The wheels skid as the motorcycle keeps sliding toward the busy street. Self-preservation gives him only one option. He lays the bike down on the street.

Joe ends up with a wrecked motorcycle, assorted cuts and bruises, and NINE TICKETS. Each ticket carries a fine of up to $200, not to mention what those tickets will do to his insurance.

Joe ends up a sadder, poorer, but wiser man. (His lawyer ends up richer.)

1.2 *Seat Belts.* The law requires that the driver and front-seat passenger wear seat belts and shoulder harnesses. After you've stopped, DON'T RELEASE YOUR SEAT BELT UNTIL the officer has approached your window and seen it or orders you out of the car. If you release it as soon as you stop, you may be ticketed for NO SEAT BELT, because the officer did not see you wearing it. This ticket carries a fine of not less than $25 or more than $50.

1.3 *Identification.* Be prepared to present your valid driver's license. If you have a valid license but don't have it with you, DON'T PANIC. A ticket for no driver's license will be dismissed when you show the license to the appropriate court. If you have an expired license or never had a driver's license, the fine is any amount up to $200. Possession of an altered license or false license can mean big trouble (see § 1.82 for further information).

SPECIAL NOTE: Almost all automobile insurance policies REQUIRE that you have a current, valid license for the policy to be effective. If you have let your license expire, your insurance may not be in effect until you renew the license. A lost or stolen license can be replaced upon payment of a small fee. Suspended licenses are treated elsewhere (§ 1.81).

1.4 *Proof of Insurance.* All drivers (Texas residents and nonresidents alike) must carry proof of liability insurance and present that proof upon demand. If you are stopped, it will be demanded. In Texas, most insurance companies provide a billfold-size proof of policy card complete with effective dates. It is also acceptable to present a copy of the policy. If you don't have proof with you, you will be ticketed. If you later prove that you had a policy in effect at the time of the ticket, the court will dismiss this ticket. Sometimes a small fee is charged. The punishment, if you had no insurance in effect, is as follows:

> *First offense:* $175–$350 fine, local court costs, and $75 state court costs.
> *Second offense:* $350–$1,000 fine, local court costs, and $75 state court costs; in addition, you must obtain insurance and keep it in effect for two years or have your license and car registration suspended.

More about specific types of insurance later in this book (see §§ 1.34–1.49).

1.5 *Warrant Check.* The police officer will check your name, date of birth, and license number for any outstanding warrants via computer. Any tickets issued by a Texas highway patrolman that are overdue and unpaid will be in the computer. Some tickets issued by city police in other cities will also be listed, if overdue and unpaid. Overdue tickets from the city police of the city in which you are being stopped will also be listed.

If any warrants appear, you will be arrested and must either pay the fine or post a bond (more about bonds in § 1.21 and § 2.4) to be released on both the ticket with the warrant AND the new ticket the officer has just issued to you.

1.6 *Don't Argue with the Officer.* If the officer asks for an explanation, give it in a calm voice and a respectful manner. However mad you may be at the officer, it is STUPID to argue or be disrespectful. Most officers will be courteous, but even if the officer is not courteous, stay cool, calm, and polite. Remember, like it or not, the officer is in charge of the situation. The use of profane, vulgar, or obscene language *or gestures* is a violation of the disorderly conduct law. YOU CAN BE ARRESTED for breaking it. The momentary pleasure you get from cursing or gesturing is *not worth a night in jail* and a fine of up to $500 (more about disorderly conduct in § 2.25).

1.7 *Sign the Ticket.* Signing the ticket in Texas is NEVER a plea of guilty. It is only your promise to contact the court (the ticket uses the legal term *appear*) within the specified time limit (usually 10 days). If you refuse to sign the ticket, you are refusing to contact the court on your own. The officer has no choice but to arrest you. To get out of jail you will have to post a bail bond or pay the fine (see §§ 1.21 and 2.4).

1.8 *Mistakes on the Ticket.* Mistakes on the ticket DO NOT usually result in a ticket being dismissed. A misspelled name, the wrong date, time, sex, license number, vehicle description, or location DOES NOT get a ticket dismissed. The only way to use these errors to your advantage is to go to trial. At that trial, when cross-examining the officer, you can point out the errors for the jury. You point out to the jury that if the officer made mistakes on the ticket, maybe he or she was mistaken about the offense, too.

1.9 *Showing the Speed Locked-In on Radar.* The officer DOES NOT have to show you the speed you are accused of going locked-in on radar. No matter where this old rumor started, let it end here.

1.10 *Tickets for Expired Inspection Sticker or Vehicle Registration.* Some courts will dismiss these tickets for a $10 fee upon proof of your renewal of whichever had expired.

1.11 *Which Law Enforcement Agency Gave You the Ticket.* The Texas Highway Patrol (also known as the Department of Public Safety or DPS) issues green tickets. They can ticket you anywhere. As their name implies, they most often give tickets on the highway. Normally, a DPS ticket goes to the justice of the peace court to be decided. City and town police give tickets in a variety of sizes and colors. They normally ticket inside the city and town limits, *but* they can follow you outside the city. *Don't* think you can escape them by leaving their city or town. City or municipal courts usually try police tickets. County sheriff's deputies do less traffic enforcement than the DPS or city police. Deputies have the authority to do traffic enforcement, if they so choose. Their tickets also vary in size and color and normally go to the justice of the peace court.

Knowing which agency gave you the ticket simplifies things, if you lose the ticket. You will know which court to contact.

1.12 *Time Limit on the Ticket.* By law, the time limit must be at least 10 days. Some courts allow you more time. Read the ticket. Although the ticket uses the word *appear* before the court, this is a legal term. It does not necessarily mean that you must appear in person. For most courts you can "appear" by telephone or by letter. Whatever way you choose to do it, CONTACT THE COURT. In small towns, you may talk directly to the judge. In the larger cities, you'll talk to the court clerk or prosecutor. If you want more than 10 days to come up with the money, most courts will give you extra time, within reason, if you contact the court *before* the 10 days are up. Remember, asking for extra time is asking a *favor*, which the court does not have to grant, SO BE POLITE.

1.13 *Informally Handling the Ticket.* Many people say they just want "to talk to the judge," not have a real trial. Some judges will allow this. Some will not. Justices of the peace are more likely to allow it, but not all of them will. This "informal talk" seldom results in a ticket dismissal. It is unreasonable to expect the judge to dismiss a ticket based only on your story. It is only fair that he or she hears what the officer has to say, too. That is what a trial is for. Some people want this "informal talk" to admit they were guilty but had a "good reason" for breaking the law. The most you can reasonably expect a judge to do in those circumstances is reduce the fine. Ask for the "informal talk" if you want to, but don't be surprised if it is not granted or does not turn out the way you expected.

1.14 *Failure to Appear.* If you fail to contact the court ("appear") within the time limit, the judge can issue a *second ticket*, called a "failure to appear." Normally you will be notified of this by mail sent to the address on your driver's license. This ticket carries a fine of $0–$200. The amount is up to the judge. Generally speaking, there is no legally acceptable reason for failing to appear, so CALL THE COURT ON TIME. "I forgot" or "I lost the ticket" cuts no ice with most judges.

1.15 *Warrant for Your Arrest.* If you ignore the "failure to appear" notice or if the judge decides not to issue a "failure to appear" ticket, he or she issues a warrant for your arrest. This can be served on you by an officer coming to arrest you if you're nearby. If you are not, the judge enters it in the statewide computer and waits for you to be stopped for something else (see § 1.5, for what happens next).

1.16 *Entering a Plea.* You can make three pleas:

    1. *Guilty:* You automatically enter this plea if you pay the ticket or attend defensive driving school (DDS), UNLESS you tell the clerk or judge that you wish to plead NO CONTEST. A guilty plea is an admission of guilt.

    2. *No contest:* Also known by the Latin phrase *nolo contendere*, this plea DOES NOT admit guilt but says that you don't want to have a trial (contest) on the matter. It allows you to pay the fine or attend DDS *but* does not admit guilt. Use this plea in all accident cases. This is important, if you were not 100 percent at fault in the accident. For a further explanation, see the entry at accidents (§ 1.58).

3. *Not guilty:* You enter this plea if you want to have a trial on the issue of fault. In most courts, you will be required to post a bond to guarantee that you'll show up at the trial (see more about "appearance bonds" in § 1.21). The trial will be held in the county or town where you got the ticket. You have the option to have a trial before the judge alone or before a jury. The trial will normally be at some time in the future weeks or months.

1.17 Options When You Have Received a Ticket.   You generally have three options:

1. *Pay the fine.*

2. *Attend defensive driving school (DDS).*

3. *Go to trial.*

These are explained below.

1.18 Fine on Tickets.   With a few exceptions such as the "no insurance ticket," most traffic tickets carry a fine of $0–$200. The exact amount is up to the judge, or if you go to a jury trial, to the jury. Generally speaking, you will be required to pay the fine set by the judge all at once. The law does not provide for payments in installments, although you may find some judges willing to allow this.

1.19 Defensive Driving School (DDS).   If you possess a valid Texas driver's license and have not attended DDS in the last year, you may request that you be allowed to attend DDS, instead of paying the fine. If the judge agrees, you pay a fee of about $10 to the court. The school itself costs about $25. The ticket DOES NOT go on your record for any purpose. The school consists of two four-hour sessions. A list of approved schools can be obtained from the court of the town where you intend to go to school.

Remember, DDS CANNOT be used to take care of a ticket for reckless driving, no proof of insurance, or a speed of more than 25 miles over the posted speed limit.

Some judges will require you to sign a sworn affidavit, stating that you have not attended DDS in the last year and are not currently enrolled to take DDS to take care of another ticket.

Usually, you may get court permission to attend DDS over the phone, through the mail, or in person. Certain courts require that you appear in person to request DDS. If you are unable to do so, you will not get permission to attend DDS for that ticket.

1.20 *Go to Trial.* Generally speaking, municipal courts hear trials on tickets issued inside the city or town limits, usually by city police officers. Justice courts hear trials on tickets issued outside the city limits but inside the county limits, usually by the highway patrol (green ticket). The municipal judge is either elected or appointed and is usually a lawyer in larger towns and cities. The justice court judge is the justice of the peace and always elected. The justice of the peace is usually not a lawyer, except in some major metropolitan areas.

1.21 *Appearance Bond.* In either court, if you ask for a trial, you will usually be asked to post an appearance bond. This is either cash or a "paper bond," which is a promise to pay money if you fail to appear for trial. When you appear for trial, the cash will be refunded (with no interest). If you fail to appear, the cash bond will be forfeited, and you will be found guilty on the ticket. The bond money becomes your fine. If a "paper bond" was used, a warrant for your arrest is issued. You as principal, and the two sureties who cosigned the bond with you, must pay the amount of the bond to the court.

"Paper bonds" are somewhat difficult and sometimes costly to obtain for traffic tickets. You can pay a professional bondsman a nonrefundable fee to post the paper bond on your behalf, or you can locate a blank appearance-bond form yourself. Then you find two people willing to cosign the bond with you. By signing, they are saying that they'll pay to the court the cash amount of the bond if you don't show up for trial. The bond must be approved by the judge of the appropriate court. On the whole, the cash bond is usually much easier to do.

The amount of the bond is up to the judge. It does not usually exceed $200 and is sometimes only the amount of the fine.

1.22 *Court Reporter.* A court reporter records everything said in a trial. This reporter is available in some municipal courts and is optional. A recording of the trial is useful in some types of appeal but generally *not* necessary for appeal to county court.

Judge or Jury?

Which kind of trial is right for you? If you hire a lawyer, let the lawyer choose. If you are representing yourself, there are many factors that you should consider. Here are a few to think about.

1.23 *Judge.*
ADVANTAGES:

1. Trial is usually set quicker.

2. Usually the judge will not increase the amount of the fine set before trial, if he or she finds you guilty after the trial.

3. A person representing himself or herself may feel less intimidated before a judge than a six-person jury.

DISADVANTAGES:

1. In many jurisdictions, the judge may know the officer.

2. The judge may hold you more strictly to the letter of the law than a jury would.

1.24 *Jury.*
ADVANTAGES:

1. Except in very small towns, the jury members seldom know you or the officers.

2. The jury may tend to put themselves in your place and not judge you so strictly by the letter of the law.

3. In justice courts, you can choose to have the jury assess ONLY guilt or innocence, not the fine. If you leave the fine amount to the judge, it will probably be the same as it was before trial.

4. Six people must believe you are guilty rather than just one.

DISADVANTAGES:

1. In municipal court, juries assess guilt or innocence AND the fine. There is no option to have the judge set the fine. The jury can be told only that the fine is from $0 to $200. They can't be

told the judge's usual fine. You run the risk that the jury might set a higher fine than the judge did, if the jury finds you guilty.

2. The average age of a jury will usually be that of your parents. Older adults are sometimes more skeptical of the truthfulness of young adults than a judge might be.

1.25 *Do You Need a Lawyer?* This is, after all, a *real trial.* An attorney will be there to represent the city or county. Naturally, you would have a better chance of winning if you hired a lawyer. It may not cost as much as you think. Check the cost by calling several attorneys. If it is beyond your budget, do not panic. Although you are not entitled to a court-appointed lawyer on a Class C misdemeanor, you may be able to defend yourself adequately. Usually, the judge will help you follow the correct procedure. Follow his or her instructions and stay polite.

1.26 *Will the Officer Show Up?* Yes, most of the time. In Dallas or Houston, there is a greater chance that the officer won't show, and your case will then be dismissed.

1.27 *Some Basics If You Represent Yourself.* For further information, see Table 1.

1. *Stay polite:* STAY POLITE. STAY POLITE. Nobody likes a smart aleck. If you lose your temper, you will usually lose your case. Make your case more believable by showing mature behavior.

2. *Proper dress and appearance:* The judge or jury will get their first impression of you from your appearance. Do the most to make that a good one. Dress as you would for church. Guys, that means at least a sports jacket, and leave the earring at home. Everyone, leave the hard rock T-shirts at home with the holey jeans. Subdue any unusual hairstyles. If your hair is purple, change it. You can always redye it after the trial. Rightly or wrongly, the more serious your dress and demeanor, the more likely the judge or jury will believe you. Proclaiming your alternate lifestyle belongs in a different arena. Here, it will only hurt you.

3. *Who goes first?* The prosecution.

4. *Selecting a jury:* STAY POLITE. You want a fair jury that doesn't know you or anyone else involved in the trial. If the main witness against you is an officer, ask if anyone is married

Table 1
Outline of Procedure in a Civil or Criminal Trial

Step	Procedure
1	Select a jury (omit this step in a nonjury trial).
2	The chosen jury is empaneled and sworn in by the judge.
3	The trial begins.
4	Opening argument by prosecution or plaintiff (optional).
5	Plaintiff or prosecution calls and questions the first witness.
6	Respondent or defendant cross-examines (questions) the first witness.
7	Plaintiff or prosecutor calls and questions each witness. Respondent or defendant cross-examines each witness in turn.
8	The plaintiff or prosecution has presented all witnesses and evidence and ends its case, called "resting" its case.
9	The respondent or defendant makes his or her opening statement or argument (optional).
10	The respondent or defendant calls and questions his or her first witness.
11	The plaintiff or prosecutor cross-examines (questions) the witness.
12	The respondent or defendant calls and questions each witness in turn. The plaintiff or prosecutor cross-examines each one.
13	The judge reads to the jury the law to be applied on the case (omit if no jury).
14	Closing arguments. The plaintiff or prosecutor goes first, and the respondent or defendant goes second. Sometimes the plaintiff or prosecutor gets a final few minutes of rebuttal time.
15	The jury retires to consider its verdict (omit if no jury).
16	The judge or jury gives the verdict.

to, related to, or close friends with the officer. That person might tend to believe the officer rather than you. Be sure all potential jurors drive. On a traffic offense you want only drivers on the jury. You have the right to "strike" (mark through) the names of three jurors on the jury list without giving a reason. The prosecution also has three strikes. The first six jurors not struck off the list will become the jury.

5. *The trial begins:* The trial will start with the prosecutor questioning the officer. DON'T INTERRUPT! Lawyers sometimes do with an objection, but you won't know what to object to, so stay quiet.

6. *Cross-examination:* You may ask the officer questions when the prosecutor is finished. STAY POLITE. Ask anything necessary to make the situation clearer. Be careful if you disagree with the officer's answer. Calling him or her a *liar* will NOT make points with the jury. You'll get your chance to talk later.

7. *Your testimony:* You cannot be made to testify if you don't want to, BUT in a traffic ticket case you may have no other way to tell your side of the story. If you do testify, tell your story as logically and briefly as you can. There will usually be a blackboard that you can use, if necessary. If you contradict the officer, use words like "The officer must be mistaken," *not* "He [or she] is a liar."

8. *The prosecutor's turn:* The prosecutor will cross-examine you when you have finished with your story. STAY POLITE.

9. *Other witnesses:* If you have witnesses, they must appear in court *in person.* A written statement will not be allowed. You'll question the witness first, and the prosecutor will cross-examine after.

10. *The verdict:* Either the jury retires to the jury room to reach a verdict, or, if there is no jury, the judge decides.

1.28 *Appeals.* Appeals of a guilty verdict from the justice court and many municipal courts go to the county court for a new trial. I recommend that you do not attempt this without a lawyer.

1.29 *Which Option Is Right for You?* It depends. Factors to consider include the following:

1. How many tickets have you had before? If this is your very first ticket, paying it may be the cheapest way out. If this is your fourth ticket in 12 months and you pay it, you will lose your license, not to mention what it will do to your insurance (see notes on license suspension in § 1.80).

2. Where did you get the ticket? If you got the ticket 400 miles from home, it may not be realistic to return for a trial. If you got the ticket in your hometown, you may want to go to trial.

3. Are you eligible for defensive driving school? See § 1.19 on requirements of eligibility for DDS. This is a good way to keep a ticket off your record.

4. How much is the fine?

5. What is the ticket for? In some cases, there is no wiggle room. If you are accused of driving with only one headlight, you either were or you weren't. The judge or jury is presented with only one fact issue. In this case, most people admit to driving with one headlight but want to give an explanation. *No explanation can make you not guilty.* (It might lessen the fine.) The same is true for expired registration or inspection sticker. If you are accused of speeding, you may have some "wiggle room." You may convince a jury that the officer made a mistake.

6. How fast does the ticket allege you were going? The higher the speed, the less likely a judge or jury will believe that it is a mistake. A speed of 80 m.p.h. or above reduces your chance of winning at trial to zero.

7. What kind of vehicle do you drive? Fair or not, juries tend to disbelieve people who drive sports cars, souped-up cars, or motorcycles.

8. Are you already on probation for another ticket or for license suspension?

If you are, one conviction during the term of probation will probably get your probation revoked. You'd better hire a lawyer for a trial or represent yourself at trial.

SPECIAL NOTE: If you ask for a trial, you can change your mind and pay the fine or ask for DDS anytime until the beginning of the trial. If you go to trial and are found guilty, the judge *may* allow you to attend DDS if you are eligible, BUT DON'T COUNT ON IT. It is up to the judge's discretion.

1.30 *When Most Tickets Are Given.* Most tickets are given between 11:00 P.M. and 5:00 A.M. Be especially law abiding during that time.

True Story Number Two

Joe Anyone is driving his car late at night. The streets are quiet, with almost no traffic. In fact, only one other vehicle is around. Joe has a red light as he approaches the intersection. He gets in the far right lane to make a right turn. He glances at the other car, sees that it is far enough away for safety, and only slows his car before turning, rather than stopping completely.

You guessed it. That other car was the police. The red lights go on. Joe, remembering what happened with his motorcycle, stops immediately. This time he is going to be smart and keep trouble to the minimum. He gives the officer his driver's license and proof of insurance, as requested. While Joe is waiting for the ticket, he says nothing, but his thoughts are boiling. He's thinking how stupid this all is. He could have avoided a ticket and fine by coming to a complete stop. It would have been so easy. The few seconds saved by not stopping aren't worth the fine. What will the ticket do to his insurance? He's really kicking himself mentally.

The officer gives him the ticket to sign. He does so and returns the pad to the officer. The officer gives Joe his copy of the ticket and starts to walk away.

Joe can't hold it in any longer. He starts cursing, mad at himself, the whole situation and maybe a little mad at the officer. The officer hears it and doesn't like it. The officer assumes it is all addressed to him. Now, he's mad, too.

He arrests Joe for vulgar language in a public place. Joe goes directly to jail. Now Joe is really mad at himself. This "disorderly conduct" charge carries a fine of up to $500. The worst part is being arrested and jailed. To get out of jail, Joe must plead guilty and pay the fine (giving himself a criminal record) or plead not guilty and pay a bailbondsman to get out. Then he must ask for a trial or plead guilty and pay a fine. The time in jail is worse than the expense. Once again, Joe is sadder, much poorer, and hopefully, a little wiser.

1.31 *In Case You've Forgotten, Some Basic Traffic Rules.*

1. Left turns always yield, except on a green arrow.

2. Most cities have an ordinance making a U-turn illegal at a stoplight, regardless of whether a sign is posted or not.

3. Stop signs mean a complete, dead stop. (Cyclists, that means one foot on the ground.)

4. If making a right turn on a red light, stop completely.

5. Backing cars ALWAYS yield.

1.32 *Tickets in Other States.* In times past, you could ignore a ticket you were given in another state. No longer. Most states are now members of the Interstate Compact. This means, if you ignore the ticket, the ticketing state will contact your home state. Your home state will notify you that if you don't resolve the out-of-state ticket, your license WILL BE SUSPENDED! As a practical matter, this means you have to pay the ticket, since it is usually very difficult to return for trial. DDS *does not* work for an out-of-state ticket.

1.33 *Tickets and Insurance.* The effect a ticket has on your insurance depends on the type of insurance policy you have and your insurance company. If you can't find on your policy the name of any of the types listed below, ask your insurance agent. A ticket taken care of by DDS or probation can't be used against you.

Generally speaking, if you have:

1. *State Set Rate Plan with deviations up or down:* Individual tickets *as they occur* do not automatically increase the premium. However, if you get enough tickets in a policy period (three is a common number), your company may refuse to renew your policy at the same rate. Accidents *can* increase the premium (see § 1.47 for further information).

2. *Texas Insurance Plan (high or assigned risk):* When you have a bad driving record, are under age 25, or have no previous driving history in the United States, this may be the only kind of policy you can get. It is expensive, and each ticket increases the expense (see § 1.48 for further information).

SPECIAL NOTE: If you are on a policy with your family, then the insurance company counts the entire family's tickets *together* for purposes of cancellation or premium increases.

If you are legally entitled to possess a driver's license, you are entitled to insurance coverage, but it may not be with the company you want or at the price you want to pay.

Vehicular Insurance

This section is intended as a basic look at insurance for cars and motorcycles. For specifics you should read your insurance policy contract. Many contracts are written in plain English. For further information, contact your insurance agent or the State Board of Insurance. For information on making a claim on your insurance, see the sections on traffic accidents (§§ 1.62–1.78).

1.34 *How to Find Insurance.* Shop the yellow pages of your telephone directory. You will find insurance companies and insurance agents listed. The insurance agent sells the policy to you. He or she does not process the claims or make the rules. He or she is either an independent agent who represents several different companies or a tied agent who only represents a single company.

Shop around for the best price. Be sure that you give accurate information on your driving record, age, and the year, model, and make of your car. All of that information is used to fix the cost of your policy.

The State Board of Insurance sets the maximum rate, but some companies offer coverage for less.

1.35 *What State Law Requires.* The state requires that you have your vehicle covered by a liability policy (see § 1.38) with coverage amounts of $20,000/$40,000/$15,000, commonly referred to as the 20/40/15 limit. This is the *least* amount of insurance you can carry.

What does 20/40/15 mean? The first two figures, 20/40, mean that in any accident the total amount of insurance coverage available to be paid for personal injuries is $40,000. The total amount that will be paid to a single person for injuries in that accident is $20,000. If you have this minimum coverage, the following examples will help you understand how it works:

1. Only one person is injured and the bills add up to $30,000. Your policy will pay only $20,000 to one person, even though your total policy limit for one accident is $40,000. YOU ARE PERSONALLY RESPONSIBLE FOR THE REMAINING $10,000.

2. Three people are injured and the total bill is $60,000. Your policy will pay only $40,000 divided among the three injured people and no more than $20,000 to any one person. YOU ARE RESPONSIBLE FOR THE REMAINING $20,000.

The figure 15 refers to property damage. This usually means the other vehicle but also means the light pole or fence or house that you struck. The policy will pay a maximum of $15,000 for property damage. Any amount due over that must come from you.

Because potential medical bills can be so expensive and because car repair and value is so high, MOST COMPANIES RECOMMEND THAT YOU CARRY COVERAGE WITH HIGHER LIMITS to protect yourself.

1.36 *Premium.* A premium is the price you pay to obtain an insurance policy—in other words, its actual cost to you.

1.37 *Deductible.* Some types of insurance coverage have a "deductible." This means you pay the damage yourself until the deductible amount is reached. The insurance company pays the rest. If your deductible is $250, then you pay the first $250 of any accident. The higher the deductible, the lower the policy premium (price). A liability policy has no deductible. There are deductibles on uninsured motorist, collision, fire, theft, and vandalism coverage.

Types of Coverage

1.38 *Liability.* To comply with state law, you must have this coverage. This coverage means that if you are at fault in an accident and the other party is injured or has property damage, your insurance will pay for the other party's actual damage and injuries up to the limits of your policy. Liability DOES NOT pay for your own injuries or damage to your vehicle. Liability will pay for injuries to your passenger, if your passenger *sues* you (see § 1.41 for further information).

This is the bare minimum required by law. Even if you are trying to pay the least you can for insurance, it would be wise to add a few things to liability. The cost for some of these extra coverages is very small.

1.39 *Uninsured Motorist Coverage.* Some people are still driving around out there without insurance, even though it is against the law. If an uninsured motorist is at fault in your accident and you only have liability coverage, you have a problem. Technically, the uninsured motorist should pay for your damages out of his or her own pocket, but you can't get blood out of a turnip. Many uninsured motorists have nothing. You may be left to repair your own damage, while you try to collect from the uninsured motorist.

If you have uninsured motorist insurance coverage, your problem is solved. You pay the deductible ($250 is common), and your insurance coverage pays the rest. Then the insurance company tries to collect from the uninsured motorist. This coverage is valuable and adds little to the cost of the policy. The Texas legislature thinks so highly of it that they passed a law requiring you to sign a paper saying you *don't* want this coverage, if you get only liability coverage. I recommend that you do get uninsured motorist coverage.

1.40 *Underinsured Motorist Coverage.* Sometimes linked with uninsured motorist coverage, this coverage takes care of you in a different circumstance. If the motorist who hit you has insurance but has only the statutory limits, 20/40/15 (see § 1.35), and your injuries total $30,000, then his or her insurance will pay you only $20,000, the policy limit. The underinsured motorist himself or herself owes you the remaining $10,000. Could you pay someone $10,000? Probably he or she can't either. If you have underinsured motorist coverage, you claim on *it* for the additional $10,000. The company then seeks to recover from the underinsured motorist. Adding this coverage costs very little.

1.41 *Personal Injury Protection (PIP).* This optional coverage will pay for personal injury to you or your passengers, when you are at fault in an accident. It is available in such specific amounts of coverage as $2,500, $5,000, or $10,000 per accident. This is the only type of vehicle insurance coverage that covers your own injuries, if you are at fault. Your own medical insurance will cover you in most accidents, so you may elect not to add this coverage, even though it is very cheap.

SPECIAL NOTE: You may want to have this coverage for your passengers. Your own medical policy will *not* cover them, unless they are family members covered by your medical insurance policy. If they are not, there is no personal injury coverage on your car insurance, UNLESS they sue you in court. In that case, your liability coverage pays. The liability coverage *only pays* if there is a lawsuit. Without PIP, you force your friends to sue you to be covered by your insurance.

1.42 *Collision.* This is also optional, unless you are still paying for your car. If you are, the terms of your loan agreement or note REQUIRE that you have this coverage. Collision coverage pays to repair your car when you are at fault in an accident. There is a deductible ($250 is common).

1.43 *Fire, Theft, and Vandalism.* This is just what it says. If your car is damaged in one of those ways or by a natural disaster (like a tornado), this coverage pays. There is a deductible, usually smaller than the other deductibles ($100 is common).

1.44 *What Kind of Coverage Is Right for You?* If you are still paying on the car, you *must* carry all of the above, except for PIP. If your car is paid for, you are only required to carry liability. I suggest you find out the cost of the various additional coverages and then decide. Remember, if you have only liability coverage and your car is stolen, damaged, or never recovered, you are out the money.

1.45 *What Is Not Covered?* Read the policy. It lists specific exclusions. Unlicensed drivers are not covered. People with a *learner's permit* are covered *only* if a licensed driver is in the front seat. Automobile policies do not cover motorcycles, off-road vehicles, and so forth. A basic policy does not cover you if you use your car in your business all the time. It *does cover* you driving to and from work. If you use your car in business for more than this, you must tell the insurance company, and they will draw up a policy to cover you. You are not covered if you *rent* your car to someone. You are not covered in the event of war or riot. YOU ARE NOT COVERED IF YOU DRIVE IN MEXICO.

1.46 *Unexpected Coverage.* Your policy does cover you if you drive someone else's car. Your policy also covers you if you lend (not rent) your car to a licensed driver. Your policy covers you if you rent a car.

Types of Plans

As I mentioned earlier when I was talking about the effect of traffic tickets on insurance costs, two insurance plans are common in Texas. Your record, or for a family policy, the entire family's record, determines the plan for which you qualify.

Tickets that you take care of by attending defensive driving school CANNOT be used to increase insurance rates under either plan.

1.47 *State Set Rate Plan with Deviations.* Most drivers over age 25 have this type of plan. The base rate (premium) is set by the state. Companies consider what type of risk you are and then give you a discount on the state rate (deviation downward) or add to the state base rate (deviation upward). If you are over 25 and have no tickets on your record for the last three years, you may get a deviation on your premium for as much as 25 percent less than the state rate. If you have a child who becomes a driver at age 16, even though that 16-year-old has no tickets, you will lose that 25 percent downward deviation and probably receive an upward deviation above the state rate. Drivers aged 16–25 statistically have a higher risk of accidents, so the insurance costs more.

Individual tickets cannot cause your premium to increase. However, if you or your family receive enough tickets within a short time period, your insurance company may refuse to renew your policy at the same rate. There will be an upward deviation in the new premium. "Enough" tickets may be as few as three in

12 months. The company determines how many are "enough." Remember, it doesn't mean three tickets per person but a three-ticket total for all of those in your family covered under the plan.

You are also penalized for accidents and driving while intoxicated convictions.

1.48 *Texas Insurance Plan (High or Assigned Risk).* The state does NOT set rates on this type of policy. If you have a bad driving record, have no previous driving history in the United States, or are considered a bad risk for any other reason, this may be the only type of insurance you can buy. The premium can be 75 to 200 percent *higher* than the state set rate. Shop around. The rates will vary greatly from company to company.

Each ticket, accident, or DWI conviction increases the policy premium (cost).

After three years, if you have kept a good record and you have reached age 26, you can obtain insurance at the state rate (see § 1.47 above).

1.49 *State Board of Insurance.* Any complaints about insurance agents or companies can be made in writing to:

> Texas State Board of Insurance
> Claims and Complaints
> 1110 San Jacinto
> Austin, Texas 78701-1998
> In Austin: 463-6515
> All others: 1-800-252-3439

Traffic Accidents

If you drive a car, sooner or later you'll be involved in an accident. Most accidents are minor with only property damage and no injuries. They can still be a pain to deal with, especially if you've never dealt with one before. Here is some basic information on how the system works.

1.50 *Stop!* The first rule in any accident is to STOP. DO NOT leave the scene. The law requires that you stay. Failure to do so can result in a fine of up to $200, if property damage is less than $200. If property damage is more than $200, the fine is $0–$2,000 and jail time of up to six months. Leaving, if there is a death, is a felony, punishable by imprisonment not to exceed five years or jail time not to exceed one year and/or a fine not to exceed $5,000. You are an adult now. A mature person accepts the consequences of his or her actions, even if they are painful.

It is much worse to hit and run than it is just to stop after the hit.

1.51 *Moving the Vehicles.*   Ideally, you should not move the vehicles. The investigating officer can then see the actual scene to determine fault. In the real world, this may not be practical. Leave the cars where they are if you can safely do so. The law states that on a freeway, you should move to the nearest off-ramp or service road if possible.

1.52 *Warning! Warning! Warning!*   When driving past an accident scene, be especially careful. It is only human to want to look and see what happened, but it is very dangerous. Everyone is looking at the accident instead of paying attention to his or her own driving. You don't want to have an accident while gawking at one that has already happened.

1.53 *To Call or Not to Call the Police.*   State law requires that the officers be called in any accident where anyone is hurt or killed or if the cars cannot be driven away. Violation of this law results in a ticket with a fine of up to $200.

State law requires that if you do not call the police, but anyone was hurt or killed or property damage was more than $500, you must file a written accident report with the Texas Department of Public Safety (DPS) within 10 days of the accident. Failure to do so can result in another fine of up to $200.

Officers will investigate any accident with at least $500 damage or more.

When in doubt, play it safe—call the police. Agreeing with the other party not to call means nothing. If the other party gets cold feet and calls the police later, you'll be ticketed for "leaving the scene." You cannot agree to break the law.

It is easier to collect damages if the officers were called and gave the other party a ticket for causing the accident.

True Story Number Three

Joe Anyone stops at a stoplight, waiting for it to turn green. While it is still red, a car plows into him from the rear. Mr. Careless Driver jumps out of his car and apologizes. He says that it was entirely his fault (true) and that his insurance will pay for everything (also true). The damage is not too great, and no one is hurt. Mr. Driver gives Joe all kinds of information including name, address, insurance company information, and so forth. Then Mr. Driver says, "Let's not call the officers. We'll have to wait forever." (Besides, Mr. Driver will surely be given a ticket for following too closely.)

Joe agrees. Later, Joe begins to worry. What if Mr. Driver's insurance won't pay because the officers weren't called? (*Not ever true!!*) In a panic, Joe decides to report the accident himself, several days late. An officer comes to the house to get the details. He asks Joe how much damage was done to his car. Joe says $600. Since it was more than $500, the officer promptly gives Joe a ticket for leaving the scene of an accident without reporting it. He then locates Mr. Driver and gives him the same ticket, plus one for following too closely.

It's always better to call the officers to the scene rather than call them later.

1.54 *Private Property.* In spite of what you have heard, police CAN investigate accidents that occur on private property, if that private property is used by the general public—this means parking lots at malls, grocery stores, and shopping centers, but not parking lots at apartments or private driveways.

1.55 *Insurance Company Myth.* Some people believe that if you don't call the officers to the accident scene, you can't collect on your insurance. WRONG! You can collect from an insurance company whether the police make an accident report or not. It is still better to call the officers. Insurance companies urge you to obey the law.

1.56 *Get the Names of Witnesses.* In some accidents, witnesses are crucial in determining fault. The best witness is someone who is a stranger to both parties in a good position to see the accident. Ideally, the officer will get the names of witnesses. Some witnesses won't want to wait for the officer, or the officer may get busy and not get the information. Don't take a chance. Get witnesses' names, addresses, and phone numbers yourself. Witnesses in your own car are better than none. However, they will be considered likely to favor you. Their testimony is not as valuable as that of a stranger.

1.57 *Two Separate Legal Actions.* Two separate legal actions arise from a traffic accident. One is the ticket itself, a "criminal" matter; the other is the civil matter of responsibility for the damages that have occurred. This is called "liability." The two matters are independent of each other, but the ticket will have some bearing on who pays for damages.

1.58 *Who's at Fault?* The officer will ask questions, look at the accident scene, and make a decision. If the officer is able to determine fault, he or she will give a ticket. If the officer is not able to determine fault (such as in traffic light cases when each party claims a green light and there are no witnesses), he or she will give no ticket. The lack of a ticket DOES NOT necessarily mean there was no fault or equal fault. It usually means that the officer simply can't tell. Determination of fault is now up to insurance companies or the courts.

SPECIAL NOTE: Failure to receive a ticket does *not* necessarily mean you don't have to pay the other party's damages.

The "Criminal" Matter

1.59 *Accident Tickets.* You were given the ticket for the majority of the fault, such as failure to yield right of way. What do you do now? Read the §§ 1.6 through 1.29 on traffic tickets for further information. Remember to plead "no contest" or "nolo contendere" if you are going to pay the ticket. If you plead guilty, you admit 100 percent fault. If you plead no contest, you admit no percentage of fault. This leaves your insurance company free to determine what percentage of fault you had. If you've pleaded guilty, there is no wiggle room. You've accepted 100 percent fault (see § 1.62 for further information).

If you plan to go to trial on the ticket, you should hire a lawyer. Because the stakes are high on an accident ticket (not just a fine, but a likelihood of having to pay civil damages), you should maximize your chances of winning by hiring a lawyer to defend you on the ticket. Remember, the court that hears the trial on the ticket decides ONLY if you are guilty on the ticket charge. This court has NOTHING to do with deciding damages. The only penalty this court can impose is a fine of up to $200 payable to the State of Texas. HOWEVER, a finding of guilt by this court makes it more likely that you will pay damages to the other party. A finding of *not guilty* DOES

NOT necessarily mean that you don't have to pay the other party. Damages to the other party are a civil matter.

1.60 *Offsetting Penalties.* Unlike football, fault on each side DOES NOT mean that each side pays his or her own damages (unless the fault is 50%–50%). Just because the other party was speeding when you ran the stop sign does not mean that the fault is equal. The primary fault is still yours. You will still be given the ticket. In the above fact situation, the officer will usually give only one ticket—to the person with the most fault.

1.61 *Accident Report.* If a ticket was issued at the accident scene, you can get a copy of the accident report from the law enforcement agency that wrote the report. This can be done in person or by mail for a small fee several days after the accident. Insurance companies rely heavily on this report, so you should know what it says. It also gives handy information like name of the car owner, insurance company, addresses, and so forth.

CORRECTING THE ACCIDENT REPORT: If there are mistakes on the accident report, you must contact the officer that wrote the report for any changes. If you disagree with how the officer says the accident happened and you got a chance to tell the officer your version at the scene, you are unlikely to be able to get him or her to change it now. If *undisputed* facts are wrong, he or she may agree to change the report. If he or she doesn't, you can only tell the insurance company your version and hope they'll believe you.

The Civil Matter

1.62 *Comparative Negligence.* Texas recognizes that in any given accident, no one party may be 100 percent at fault. There can be, and often is, shared fault. Who has what percentage of fault is usually determined by insurance companies or the courts. This means an insurance company for the other party may decide you had 20 percent of the fault, while their insured had 80 percent. They will then offer you 80 percent of your damages. If you accept, you pay the remaining 20 percent yourself. If you do not accept, you may have to file on your own insurance or *sue* the other party.

1.63 *Contact the Insurance Company.* If you are at fault, call your agent or the company claims office to report the accident.

Let the other party know you have done so. Normally, your company will contact the other party and you need have no further involvement with the other party. If you have collision or PIP coverage, you will continue to deal with your insurance company for your own damages or injuries.

If you are the innocent party, wait a day or so for the at-fault party or his or her insurance company to call you. If you don't hear from anyone, take action. You can call the at-fault party or call directly to his or her insurance company. Those accidents with injuries or an undrivable car usually get faster treatment. *Be patient, be polite, but be persistent.* If the insurance company claims agent is to call you back, find out when. If the call does not come on time, promptly call back. Remember, *the squeaking wheel gets the grease,* or the persistent get prompter attention.

1.64 *Amount You Are Entitled To Receive in Damages.*
Nobody comes out ahead in an accident, even the party who was not at fault. Under Texas law, the measure of damages is the cost of repair, until that cost is greater than the value of the vehicle. That means, if the cost of repair is $2,000, but your car is worth only $1,500, the at-fault party is responsible for paying you only $1,500. This is called a "total." Even though the $1,500 may not get you as good a car as you had before the accident, all you are entitled to is $1,500. You *cannot* go back and sue the at-fault party for more.

SPECIAL NOTE: In a total, you give the title to your totaled car to the insurance company, which pays you the $1,500. The company is entitled to get the salvage value, if any. If you want to keep your car and add your own money to the insurance money to get it fixed, negotiate this with the insurance company. They will probably do it but will pay you only the $1,500 minus the salvage value, if any.

1.65 *How the System Works.*

1. The insurance company is notified of the accident.

2. An adjustor and/or claims agent is assigned the case. The claims agent works directly for the insurance company. The adjustor works either directly for the insurance company or for an independent adjusting company that has been hired by the insurance company.

3. Either the claims agent or adjustor takes your statement about the accident over the phone. Don't panic because it is being recorded. Just get the facts straight in your mind so that the recording makes sense.

4. The adjustor looks at your car and estimates the damages. He or she determines if it can be repaired or it is a total.

SPECIAL NOTE: Sometimes, if the damage is slight, you may be asked to get estimates to send to the insurance company, rather than an adjustor actually viewing your car.

5. If your car can be repaired, you get a rental car from the insurance company while your car is being repaired or while your car cannot be driven. If you are claiming on your own insurance rather than the other party's insurance, check your policy. You may *not* have coverage that provides a rental car. If your car is TOTALED, you are NOT ENTITLED to a rental car.

6. You choose the body shop for your repairs.

7. The car is repaired.

8. The check for the repair is made out to the body shop and you or just to you. You endorse the check.

9. You will also be asked to sign a "waiver of liability." This means that you agree that the at-fault party DOES NOT legally owe you any more money for car repair. It is printed either on the back of the check or maybe on a separate piece of paper. Usually, you MUST sign this to get the money to pay for the repair of your car.

SPECIAL NOTE 1: Remember, this waiver covers property damage only. It has nothing to do with any medical reimbursement you are owed for injuries, so it is okay to sign it, even though all of your medical has not yet been paid.

SPECIAL NOTE 2: After you sign the waiver, if the body shop finds additional damage from the accident that was missed by the adjustor, the insurance company WILL STILL PAY for it, even though you have signed the waiver. Have the body shop call the adjustor or insurance company directly to explain.

1.66 *You Disagree with the Amount Offered.* This usually occurs in two situations:

1. *Percentage of fault:* As noted in § 1.62, there can be shared fault in an accident. You may disagree with the at-fault party's insurance company that you were 20 percent at fault in the accident. If so, attempt to negotiate. If negotiation fails, you can refuse the offer to pay 80 percent of your damages. Then you claim on your own insurance for full payment minus deductible, if you have collision coverage. Your insurance company then attempts to collect. If you do not have collision coverage, you can sue the at-fault party in court and let a jury decide if you were 20 percent at fault. More about suing later.

2. *Value of your car:* The insurance company agrees that their insured was 100 percent at fault. They say your car is "totaled." They offer you $2,000 for your car. You think your car is worth more than that. First check "book value." Call the dealer for your make and model, and ask the dealer to give you "book value." If your car is older, its condition prior to the accident and the number of miles on it make a difference in value. If book value is unavailable or too low, ask used-car dealers what they would have bought such a car for and then how much they would have marked it up to sell it. An average of those two figures can be used as fair market value. Armed with this information, you may be able to convince the insurance company that your car is worth more than they offered. If not, again you can claim on your own insurance or file suit in court.

1.67 *Medical Bills.* If the other party was at fault and insured, all of your medical bills should be paid for you. If you must pay up front at the emergency room, get a receipt so that you can be reimbursed later. Some insurance companies prefer that you have bills sent directly to them for payment. Some let you pay and then reimburse you. Negotiate the method of payment, if possible.

You can settle the car damage quickly and wait on the medical. Most insurance companies expect to wait to settle the medical until your doctor releases you. If the doctor releases you but says you might need more surgery in a year, you can negotiate that with the insurance company. They'll handle it one of two ways. Either they'll simply wait to close that part of the claim until the time has passed, or they'll offer you a written agreement in which they'll agree to pay for all reasonable medical expenses arising from your injury for a set period of time. If you are not happy with the agreement offered, then you can file on your own insurance or file suit.

SPECIAL NOTE: If you are at fault in the accident, remember that your car insurance policy covers your medical only if you have PIP coverage. PIP also covers your passengers. If you do not have PIP coverage, you must claim on your medical insurance policy. If your passenger is not covered on your medical policy and there is no PIP, your passenger must claim on her or his own medical insurance policy. If the passenger doesn't have such a policy, the passenger can sue you and be covered under your liability policy.

1.68 *Medical Payments If At-Fault Party Is Uninsured.* If you have uninsured motorist coverage, you can claim on that for both property damage and medical payments. If you do NOT have this coverage, you must claim on your own medical insurance.

1.69 *Other Expenses.* If the other party is at fault, you may claim for such out-of-pocket expenses as lost wages, damaged clothing, eyeglasses, and items damaged in the car, like school books. If you are at fault and claiming on your own insurance, you are *not* likely to be reimbursed for these expenses.

1.70 *"Pain and Suffering."* This term is used to refer to the aggravation, discomfort, inconvenience, and pain that you have when you have AN INJURY. It is difficult to recover any money under this *if you were not injured.*

How much is fair? Good question. It depends on the type of injury and how painful or disabling it was.

You can negotiate this with the insurance company or *hire a lawyer* to negotiate for you.

1.71 *If the At-Fault Party Refuses to File on His or Her Insurance.* Nobody can make the at-fault party file. If the innocent party is not happy with how the at-fault party is willing to pay or if the at-fault party refuses to pay, the innocent party can sue. The insurance company of the at-fault party WILL NOT be involved in the suit at all. The company will provide no lawyer to defend and will pay no damages awarded. The at-fault party is on his or her own if he or she refuses to file the claim with the insurance company in the beginning.

If you think you are not at fault in the accident, but the other party thinks you are, it is far better to let your insurance company process the claim. If the company agrees with you and refuses to pay the other party, the company will provide a lawyer to defend you and pay any damages awarded (up to the policy limits), if you lose the lawsuit.

SPECIAL NOTE: If the at-fault party intends to pay on his or her own, he or she can do so. The innocent party DOES NOT have to accept installments, unless ordered to do so by a court judgment. If the innocent party claims on his or her uninsured motorist coverage, the insurance company will seek to collect from the at-fault party. The company may be willing to accept installments.

1.72 *Uninsured Motorist.*   If the uninsured motorist is at fault, the uninsured motorist owes the damages himself or herself. If the uninsured motorist is unable or refuses to pay, the innocent party can claim on his or her own insurance or sue.

1.73 *If You Claim on Your Own Uninsured Motorist Coverage, Can You Sue the At-Fault Uninsured Motorist to Collect Your Deductible?*   No! Once you claim on your insurance for any amount, you give up your right to sue the at-fault party to the insurance company. This is called "subrogation." The insurance company will go after the at-fault party for their own money plus your deductible. If they ever recover it, you'll get reimbursed. If they are unable to recover it, you're just out the money. If your insurance company decides NOT TO SUE the at-fault party, you may be able to get permission in writing to sue the at-fault party from your insurance company. Then you can sue for your deductible in the small claims court. You may win your suit but may never be able to collect the money (see §§ 7.4 and 7.5 in this book on small claims court for further information).

1.74 *Suing the Other Party.*   If the amount of damage is less than $5,000, you can file suit by yourself without a lawyer in small claims court. The filing fee can be an amount up to $65. Either party can bring a lawyer to small claims court if he or she is willing to pay for one (see § 7.4 on small claims court for more details).

For amounts over $5,000, you must file in a higher court, which is very difficult to do without a lawyer.

The disadvantage to suing is that it costs money and may take some time. Collecting the judgment from an uninsured party can be very difficult. Suits must be filed within two years of the date of the accident.

1.75 *Do You Need a Lawyer?*   It depends. Generally speaking, the more serious the accident, the more likely that you need a lawyer. Lawyers can negotiate for you with the other party's insurance company. Lawyers can file suit, if necessary. If you are claiming on your own insurance, you will generally not need a lawyer.

1.76 *License Suspension.*   One threat that you have to compel a person to pay you is license suspension and car registration suspension. If anyone was killed or injured or more than $1,000 worth of property damage occurred, and the at-fault party won't pay, you can file with the DPS to have his or her license suspended and car license tags removed. You can do this before you file suit. This suspension lasts two years from the date of the accident, unless you file suit by that time. If you file suit for any amount of damages and win, the suspension lasts *until you are paid.*

To do this, contact your local DPS office for instructions. Of course, if you *lose* your suit and the other party is found *not at fault,* the suspension ends.

1.77 *If You're Driving Someone Else's Car and Are At Fault.*
The car owner's insurance will pay any innocent parties. The insurance company then will come to you for reimbursement. If you are insured, your own policy will pay. If you are not, you owe the money yourself.

1.78 *Policy Limits.*   Remember, as noted in the section on insurance, the insurance company is only liable (responsible) up to the policy limits. If the at-fault party is insured only at the state limits of 20/40/15 and your injuries are $25,000 worth, the at-fault party is personally responsible for the remaining $5,000.

This is why it is recommended that you carry more than the minimum insurance (further information on policy limits is in § 1.35).

SPECIAL NOTE: If you sue, you always sue the party at fault, not his or her insurance company.

Driver's License

I presume you have obtained your driver's license from the Texas DPS with an endorsement for motorcycle, if appropriate. If you haven't, contact the DPS for instructions on how to obtain a license.

1.79 *Address.*   You should keep your current permanent address on your driver's license at all times. Remember, this means if you move, you must go in to the local DPS office to change your address on the license. You have 30 days to do so. Failure to do so can result in a ticket with a fine of up to $200.

SPECIAL NOTE TO COLLEGE STUDENTS: If you live in the dorm or in an apartment and are not self-supporting or married, this is usually considered a temporary address and your license need not be changed. You can keep your permanent home address on it.

It is very important to keep this address current because any notification from the DPS is sent to the address on your license. If your license is going to be suspended, you want to know about it. If away at college, alert Mom and Dad to forward any mail from the DPS or any government entity (such as the tiny little town where you got that unpaid speeding ticket two months ago). Legally, if the mail was sent to the address on your license, you are deemed to have gotten notice whether you actually received it or not.

1.80 *Displaying Your License.* If you are stopped by an officer for any reason, you will be asked to show your license. If you fail to do so, you will be ticketed for "no driver's license." This ticket carries a fine of up to $200 for the first offense. If you don't have your valid license with you at the time you are ticketed, don't panic. You can get the "no driver's license" ticket dismissed by showing your license to the court named on the ticket within the time allowed.

1.81 *Suspension of License.* Listed below are various reasons for a license to be suspended. The suspension is for up to one year unless noted otherwise.

1. *Habitual violator:* You receive four moving violations within 12 months or seven within 24 months, arising out of different incidents (two tickets issued in the same incident count as one; for a PROVISIONAL LICENSE holder, the limit is two or more moving violations within 12 months).

2. *Injury in an accident:* You have been responsible for an accident resulting in death, serious personal injury, or serious property damage.

3. *Driving while license suspended:* Your license has already been suspended, and you are caught driving. (This also results in immediate arrest, a fine of $100–$500, and a jail term of a minimum 72 hours to a maximum six months in jail.)

4. *Violation of license restriction:* This means if you must wear corrective lenses while driving and you get caught without them, in addition to a ticket with a fine of up to $200, your license can be suspended.

5. *Unlawful or fraudulent use of a license:* This means lending your license to someone or altering it in any way. More about altering licenses will be discussed below. This is an automatic suspension for one year for the first offense.

6. *Driving while intoxicated:* This suspension is for not less than 90 days or more than 365 days for a first offense. The penalty increases for subsequent DWI's.

7. *Refusal to take the breath test:* Your license is confiscated at the arrest and suspended immediately. You have 15 days to request a hearing. Even if the DWI is dismissed, the suspension is not less than 90 days if you are 21 or older. If you are under 21, the suspension is for 1 year.

8. *Scoring .10 or higher on the breath test:* If you are arrested for DWI and score a .10 or higher on the breath test, your license is automatically suspended for not less than 60 days, whether or not you are prosecuted for DWI.

9. *Being at fault in an accident for damages and failing to pay:* If you are at fault in an accident and there is *any* personal injury or property damage of $1,000 or more and you fail to pay the damages, your license may be suspended UNTIL YOU PAY. The license may be reinstated two years from the date of the accident, if no suit has been filed against you. If a suit is filed and you lose it, regardless of the amount of damages, the suspension lasts UNTIL YOU PAY.

10. *Failure to carry liability insurance:* Upon a second conviction of failure to carry liability insurance, your license may be suspended UNTIL YOU GET INSURANCE, unless you immediately obtain such insurance and provide proof to the court.

11. *Ignoring an out-of-state ticket:* If you receive an out-of-state ticket and ignore it, the odds are that you will receive a notice from the DPS. This notice tells you your license will be suspended unless you take care of the ticket (see § 1.32 for more information).

12. *Felony drug conviction:* This suspension is for 180 days.

13. *Being under 21 and convicted of DWI or drug offenses:* Your license is suspended for 12 months on a first offense. This runs concurrently with a suspension for test refusal.

In most of the above-listed situations, you are entitled to a hearing before your license is revoked. Notice for this is mailed to your license address. You may be granted probation if you are a first-time offender. There is no probation if you are suspended under (9) above. There is generally no probation under (7 or 8) above.

Your license can also be suspended for medical reasons, failure to stop and render aid in an accident, and vehicular homicide.

True Story Number Four

Joe Anyone is 21 years old. His brother, Sam, is not. Joe agrees to trade driver's licenses for the weekend. (I'll leave it to your imagination as to why Sam might want to appear to be 21.)

Joe is driving his car, upon which he has just placed oversized tires. The speedometer reads 40 m.p.h., which is the speed limit. Therefore, Joe is very surprised to be stopped by the police.

Having learned his lesson the hard way, Joe is determined that this stop will result only in a ticket. The officer asks for Joe's license. Return to Panic City. Joe only has Sam's license. Either he shows no license at all, in which case he'll get a ticket for no driver's license, or he gives the officer Sam's license.

Once again, Joe makes the wrong choice. He gives the officer Sam's license, hoping this is a routine license check and nobody will get any tickets.

The officer says to Joe, "Where are your glasses?" Joe had forgotten that Sam has to wear glasses to drive.

Joe replies, "I left them at home." The officer then says that he stopped Joe for speeding. Joe (pretending to be Sam) says that his speedometer read 40 m.p.h. The officer then tells Joe that oversized tires make the speedometer inaccurate, unless you alter the speedometer.

The officer then tickets Joe, in *Sam's* name, for speeding and not wearing glasses.

Poor Joe. Once more he has entangled himself in a costly mess. This time, he's dragged Sam into it, too.

If they keep quiet about the deception, Sam will have two tickets on his record, *plus* the DPS will move to SUSPEND his license for driving without his glasses.

If they tell the truth, Joe will get a ticket for speeding and another one for presenting a license not his own. Sam will get a ticket for allowing his license to be used by someone else. They then both face license suspension.

Joe could have avoided all of this by refusing to lend his license. There is always the chance Sam might get caught using it, and they'd then both face license suspension.

Even if Joe did trade licenses, he could have avoided most of the trouble by telling the officer that he didn't have his license with him (perfectly true). He would then have been ticketed for speeding and no license. The no-license ticket would be dropped by the court when Joe showed his valid license. Nobody would have faced suspension as long as Sam didn't get caught.

1.82 *Fake or Altered Licenses.* If you alter your own license, have it altered, purchase or use a false license, give false information to obtain a license, or lend your license to someone else, you face numerous penalties, as listed below. The penalties are even more serious if you *make* false licenses.

> **1. *Lending your license or possessing more than one license:*** Class C misdemeanor punishable by a fine up to $500. (Note: Your license is also subject to suspension.)

> **2. *False swearing on an application:*** Usually a Class C misdemeanor, punishable by a fine up to $500.

> **3. *Use of a license with false information on it:*** Class A misdemeanor punishable by up to one year in jail and a fine up to $3,000.

> **4. *Possession, use, or manufacture of a document deceptively similar to a driver's license:*** Class C misdemeanor punishable by a fine of up to $500.

> **5. *Counterfeit or forged license (note that this is different from item [4] above). Either the making, sale, or possession of a counterfeit or forged license:*** FELONY: 2 to 5 years in the state penitentiary under the Traffic Code or under the Penal Code a Third-Degree felony punishable by 2 to 20 years and/or a fine not to exceed $10,000.

Remember that your license can be suspended for one year under all of these offenses.

Because the legal drinking age is 21, many young people are tempted to do some or all of the offenses listed above. Be aware of the risks you run.

Purchase of a Car

This section is not intended to be a detailed statement on the law of contracts. It is intended to alert you to some basic laws governing contracts for the purchase of a car and other areas for concern.

1.83 *The Contract.* You have an absolute right to have a copy. Be sure to read the contract before signing. Be certain all blanks are filled in. If any alterations are made to the printed form, all parties should initial the changes.

1.84 *Three-Day Right to Cancel the Contract.* There isn't one. On certain consumer contracts a three-day right to cancel exists. The purchase of a car IS NOT one of them. Once you've signed, you have a binding contract.

1.85 *Cosigning.* A cosigner is equally responsible for making payments on the car with the first signer. This is true even though the cosigner does not have the payment book or possession of the car. If the first signer fails to pay (defaults), then the creditor can look to the cosigner for payment.

SPECIAL NOTE: The creditor seldom notifies a cosigner before repossession, acceleration of the note, and demand for payment in full is made.

If you cosign a note or have one cosigned for you, keep in touch with each other to avoid this problem.

1.86 *Acceleration of Note.* Almost all sale contracts have an acceleration clause. This clause permits the creditor to demand *payment in full* if you default on the note in any way. This includes late payments. It is far better to pay on time, but if you cannot, contact the creditor to explain. Many creditors will permit late payments if they are not too late and you have gotten permission. *However*, almost all contracts contain a statement that says that the creditor retains the right to declare a default for a late payment or other violation, even if the creditor has previously allowed late payments. In other words, the creditor can change his or her mind and without notice to you. In some situations, the car might even be repossessed, without notice, after the second late payment.

1.87 *Insurance.* The instrument that binds you to the purchase (sales contract and/or secured note) always has a clause that requires that you keep the car *fully* insured for the length of the loan. This is not "credit life insurance," which is optional, but regular comprehensive car insurance to cover you if you are involved in an accident. This is NOT liability only, but full coverage.

If you purchase comprehensive insurance, your insuror will automatically notify the creditor that you have done so. If you don't purchase insurance, the creditor gets no notice. This will trigger the creditor's purchase of its own insurance.

The creditor's policy covers *only repairs to your car* (not personal injuries or damage to the other car). The cost of this policy will be added to the note on the car. This may be done without advance notice to you. This type of policy DOES NOT meet the State of Texas requirement of liability insurance.

1.88 *When to Insure a New Car.* You should insure the car at once before you drive the car off the lot. The title does NOT have to be in your name or even properly signed for you to purchase insurance (see §§ 1.35–1.49).

1.89 *Renting instead of Owning.* It has become popular to sign a long-term rental contract for a car instead of buying the car. The rental contract is lengthy and resembles a purchase contract. Generally speaking, it requires you to carry comprehensive insurance. It also requires that you pay for mechanical repairs. In fact, you have all of the duties and responsibilities of an owner, but you don't own the car.

The potential problem in this area is in attempting to BREAK THE CONTRACT. Most people know you can't break a purchase contract, but they think a rental contract is different and not as binding. IT IS NOT DIFFERENT. Even if you voluntarily turn the car in, you still owe the remainder of the contract price. It works like a repossession. The creditor will sell the car and apply the money received to the debt. This is seldom enough to pay off the debt in full. You still owe the remainder.

Remember, a rental contract is just as binding as a sales contract.

1.90 *Deposit.* If you are required to pay one, remember, in most cases you don't get it back. If you buy the vehicle, it is credited to the purchase price. If you DON'T BUY, the seller gets to KEEP IT, as payment for having held the vehicle off the market for you and for having turned away other buyers. Be sure you understand what happens to the deposit before you pay it.

1.91 *New Cars.* All cars are covered by a warranty for a set period of time or set number of miles. A written explanation of the warranty should accompany your sales contract. Be sure you understand how to use the warranty. The main limitation in a warranty, besides the time and mileage limits, is that you must use a dealership for repairs.

1.92 *Lemon Law.*   All new cars purchased after 1 October 1983 are covered under the Texas Lemon Law.

If the same problem has been repaired four or more times by the dealer within the express warranty term or during the period of two years following the date of delivery to the purchaser, whichever is earlier, and the problem still exists;

OR

the vehicle is out of service for repair for a cumulative total of 30 or more days during that two-year period,

and

the defect substantially impairs the use and market value of the vehicle,

and

the manufacturer or distributor has been notified of the defect IN WRITING and has been given an opportunity to repair it,

the Texas Lemon Law applies.

You must request a hearing before the Texas Motor Vehicle Commission in writing, providing a copy of the letter sent to the manufacturer or distributor within 6 months of the expiration of the express warranty or 18 months after the purchase of the vehicle, whichever comes first.

The commission telephone numbers are:

(512) 505-5172 or
1-800-622-8682

The commission will hold a hearing to determine if you have met all of the requirements of the law. If you have done so, the commission will order the manufacturer to provide a new car or refund the purchase price of your car minus a reasonable allowance for your use of the vehicle.

If you are unhappy with the decision of the commission, you may sue the manufacturer, at your own expense.

Be sure to keep all of your work orders for car repairs so that you can prove how many times the car has been worked on.

SPECIAL NOTE: The Lemon Law applies *only* to NEW CARS. Even though the manufacturer's warranty transfers to a second owner, if it has not expired, the Lemon Law *does not.* The second owner has bought a "used" vehicle.

1.93 *Used Cars.* BUYER BEWARE is the watchword here. You can get a real bargain in a used car if you take simple precautions. You can buy a real headache if you do not.

The general rule is that used merchandise (including vehicles) is sold "as is." Theoretically, the seller is supposed to warn you of *known* defects. However, it is very difficult to prove that a seller *knew* of a particular defect before the sale. Unless the seller *expressly* warranties the vehicle, the seller has no responsibility for any repairs. Any such warranty should be in writing.

The seller must not make any misrepresentations about the condition of the vehicle. If you ask specific questions, the seller must answer. A direct lie, if it can be proved, can invalidate the contract. A statement of "I don't know" is difficult to prove as a lie in most cases. It is very difficult to break such a contract based on oral misrepresentations.

The safest thing to do is to take the used car to a mechanic of your choice and have him or her examine it before you buy. There may be a fee for this. A mechanic cannot spot all defects, but he or she can spot most major ones. The payment of the fee is worth it, if it saves you from a bad purchase. If the seller will not let you take the car to your own mechanic, DO NOT BUY THE CAR.

If the seller is an individual, ask to see the title to the car *before* you pay any money. This should be a "clear title," that is, with no lienholder. In some instances you can purchase a car with a title that has a lienholder, but the car can be sold *only* with the lienholder's permission. The lienholder may want payment directly from you to insure that the note gets paid off before releasing the title. NOTE: The lienholder MUST give the released title to the seller of the car, whom you must trust to sign it over to you. If the seller will give you "power of attorney" (see § 6.11), which you show the lienholder, the lienholder can send the title directly to you.

1.94 *Nonnegotiable Title.* This is stated on the face of the title if you are still paying on the car. This "title" cannot transfer ownership. Negotiable means sellable. Your creditor (lienholder) who holds the note on the car also holds the negotiable title. When the note and any other charges are paid in full, the negotiable title will be mailed to you by your creditor. In the place on the title where the lienholder's name is given, the word *released* with the date will be written. This title is now "negotiable," and you can use it to sell the car.

If you want to get a new title, with the lienholder's name removed, you may do so. To file for a new title, turn in the old one and pay a small fee at the tax assessor's office in the courthouse. In about six weeks, you'll receive the new negotiable title through the mail. Remember, a new title without the lienholder's name is optional.

1.95 *Negotiable Title.* This title will show your name as the current owner, your permanent address, and various information to identify the car. The lienholder line will be blank. A previous owner's name will be listed if there was one. There is also a signature line for you to sign on the face (front) of the title. DO THIS AT ONCE. That signature will be used for comparison when you sign on the back to sell the car.

1.96 *To Sell or Buy a Car.* The car seller must have "clear title" (that means no lienholder). If you are buying from an individual, ask to see this. If the seller doesn't have the title, DON'T BUY THE CAR. (This is usually not a problem with dealers.)

It is no longer necessary to sign the title before a notary public, even though the title may still have the place for the notary to sign on its back.

1.97 *Getting the Buyer's Name on the Title.* The buyer's name and permanent address must be filled in on the back of the old title above the seller's signature on the negotiable title. Take this to the county tax assessor's office (usually found in the county courthouse). As buyer, you will also have to fill in a new title application form stating the purchase price. The sales tax will then be assessed based on this price. You must sign this form under oath. There is a place for the seller's signature on the new title application form, but a signature is not mandatory.

In six weeks to two months, the new title will come to you in the mail. If you buy from a dealer, the dealer will do all of this for you.

As the buyer, you should transfer the title into your name IM-MEDIATELY AFTER PURCHASE. DO THIS FOR TWO REASONS:

1. The license tag renewal is mailed to the address on the title. If the title has not been reissued in your name, the reminder goes to the old owner, not to you. You may forget to renew the tags until an officer reminds you.

2. You will find out if the seller has properly signed the title right away, before the seller disappears. If you wait to transfer the title for six months, you may discover that the title is unsigned and have no way to contact the old owner. You then DO NOT HAVE TITLE TO THE CAR.

True Story Number Five

Trouble seems to run in the Anyone family. Sam Anyone likes Joe's motorcycle so well that he decides to buy one for himself. He finds an ad in the paper and pays cash for a used motorcycle. Mr. Seller gives Sam the title.

Sam has learned from Joe's mistakes. The motorcycle is registered, inspected, and insured before Sam ever rides it. Sam has also gotten his license endorsed for a motorcycle. However, he forgets one major thing. He neglects to turn in the title, pay the sales tax, and get a new title in his name.

Six months later, the license tags are about to expire. Sam realizes he must find the title to be able to get the new sticker for the tags.

The title is lost. He can't find it anywhere. The tax assessor's office tells him that the last registered owner is the only one who can file for a lost title. Sam has no idea of how to reach the old owner. He can't remember the name. When he returns to the address, the old owner has moved. The new tenants know nothing about the old owner. Sam returns to the tax office. They run a check on the motorcycle's license number and give Sam the old owner's name and the address that was on the title. It is the same address that Sam has already tried. He tries the new phone book and directory assistance, but the old owner, Mr. Seller, has disappeared.

When the tags expire, Sam can no longer ride his motorcycle. What can he do? As a last resort, Sam mails a letter to Mr. Seller at the old address, hoping that the post office will forward it to some new address. Sam gets lucky. The letter is forwarded, and Mr. Seller calls Sam.

For once, the Anyone family has a happy ending. This entire hassle could have been avoided if Sam had filed the title right away.

1.98 *Repossession.* All installment sales contracts allow repossession for failure to follow the contract. In Texas, NO NOTICE is required before repossession. As noted in the earlier paragraph on

ACCELERATION OF THE NOTE, a late payment, not previously approved by the lender, can result in repossession and payment in full being due at once. This is true even if the lender has allowed previous late payments.

1.99 *Do Not Keep the Certificate of Title in the Car.* If the car is stolen, it will allow the thief to forge your name and sell it. Keep the title in a safe place where you keep other important papers.

1.100 *Odometer.* This is the device that measures mileage on a motor vehicle. Texas law now requires that a sworn odometer statement be made by every seller in a car sale. On new title certificates there is a section on the back specifically for this. If no such section is on your title, there is a separate form for this, obtainable at the tax office at the county courthouse. A completed form, either the separate one or the one on the title itself, must be sworn to by the owner and turned in with the old title at the time of the new title application.

SPECIAL NOTE: It is no longer necessary to swear before a notary, BUT you are still swearing. If you lie, you can be prosecuted for perjury.

It is illegal to roll back the odometer to read fewer miles than the vehicle has actually been driven. This crime is punishable as follows:

> *First offense:* Jail time not exceeding two years and/or a fine up to $1,000.
> *Second offense:* Confinement in jail for not less than 30 days nor more than two years and a fine no greater than $2,000.

If you find evidence that this has been done to a car you have purchased, you should report it to the State Department of Motor Vehicles or the district attorney for the filing of criminal charges. You may also have a separate *civil* action under the Deceptive Trade Practices Act. Seek your own attorney for the civil action or file a complaint with the Texas Attorney General's Office for Consumer Affairs (see § 7.2).

Registration and Inspection

1.101 *Registration (License Tags).* In Texas you are required to renew your license tags once a year. The month in which you must renew will be the month in which you purchase a new car or, in the case of a used car, the month already noted on the car's windshield. Usually, the state will send a reminder to the name and address on the certificate of title a month before renewal is due. *However,* failure to receive a notice is NOT A LEGAL EXCUSE for driving with expired tags. If you fail to get a notice and fail to contact the local tax assessor's office for renewal, you will get a TICKET with a fine of up to $200.

Normally, renewal means paying a fee that varies with the weight of your car and receiving a new sticker to place on the car windshield. Every five years, or sooner if you desire, license tags must be replaced on your car for an additional fee. If you receive the notice by mail, you can renew by mail. You can also renew in person at the county tax assessor's office in the county courthouse.

1.102 *Number of Tags.* Texas law requires that all Texas cars have a front and rear tag and that the rear tag be lighted at night. Failure to meet either of these requirements can result in a ticket being issued that subjects you to a fine up to $200.

1.103 *Temporary License Tags.* These are the cardboard tags on new vehicles bought from dealers. They are good for only 20 DAYS. You should receive your metal tags within that time period. If you do not, contact the dealer at once. If you are caught driving with temporary tags after the 20-day period, you can be ticketed and fined up to $200. Failure to receive the metal tags is not a legal excuse.

It is ILLEGAL to transfer the tags from one vehicle to another vehicle.

1.104 *Inspection.* All vehicles must have a state inspection sticker mounted on the left front of the windshield. You have to remember *on your own,* with no notice from the state, to renew this sticker each year. The renewal can be done by any authorized mechanic. Gasoline stations and garages will prominently display a red, white, and blue sign with a map of the State of Texas on it if they do inspections. The fee for the sticker and inspection is $10.50, and the inspection takes only a few minutes. If any repairs need to be made, there will be an additional charge. A new sticker, with the month and year noted, is put on after the inspection. Repairs to bring the car in compliance with state law must be completed before the new sticker can be issued. Tires, brakes, lights, horns, mirrors, windshield wipers, front seat belts, steering, wheel assembly, exhaust system, and emission system must all be inspected.

The state gives you a five-day grace period. That means if your inspection sticker was due in November, you may get it inspected up until 5 December. Beginning on 6 December you will be ticketed. The ticket carries a fine of up to $200. Some judges will lower the fine if you produce a receipt to show that you have had the car inspected. Lowering of the fine is optional with the judge and not all judges do it.

SPECIAL NOTE: If you replace your windshield, you will have to have the car reinspected to get a new sticker. The old sticker CAN- NOT be transferred from the old windshield to the new windshield.

Car Repair

Car repair is one of the most frustrating areas of concern for consumers. It is frequently difficult to reach a satisfactory result in a complaint. Below are a few tips on how to avoid trouble and what to do if trouble occurs in spite of your best efforts.

1.105 *Seek Out a Good Mechanic.* A reliable mechanic is worth his or her weight in gold. If you find one, tell your friends about him or her so maybe he or she will stay in business. How do you find a good one? Ask friends and relations.

When you've picked out a garage, check it out BEFORE you use it. Call the local Better Business Bureau (BBB) to see if they have had any unresolved complaints on the garage. If you live in a city that has a Texas Attorney General's Office for Consumer Affairs, you can also check with them. No unresolved complaints is a good sign. However, if the garage is new, there may not have been time for complaints yet.

Match your car to the mechanic. If you have an unusual foreign car, you may not want to use "Joe Blow Mechanic." You don't want him learning about the car by working on it.

SPECIAL NOTE 1: If your car is still under warranty, you must use a dealer for the warranty to be in effect.

SPECIAL NOTE 2: If you have had your car repaired by a mechanic who guarantees his or her work, you must return the car to him or her if the problem recurs. If you are out of town, call the mechanic for instructions. Failure to do so may cancel your warranty.

1.106 *Get a Written Estimate.* If you want to know the cost of repair ahead of time, get an estimate of repair from the mechanic before you start. Be clear on whether the estimate is just a guess or is the actual cost. If the estimate is to be the actual cost, it is a *binding estimate*. Get the mechanic to write "binding" on the estimate.

Make it clear that you *must* be called to approve any additions to the estimate. On the work order estimate itself, have the mechanic note the duty to call you for additional work.

1.107 Work Order. Sometimes you may get an estimate several days or weeks before you are going to have the work done. If so, you will be asked to sign a "work order" when you bring the car in for work. Your signature authorizes the work. Be sure to keep your estimate, AND be sure everything on the estimate gets transferred to the work order. If you are going to have the work done the day you get the estimate, the estimate will probably be done on the work order itself. As noted above, be sure to get the notation "binding estimate" and "call before any additional work" WRITTEN on the work order.

1.108 Do Not Let Work Be Done on Your Car without a Written Work Order. You have no way to prove agreed prices or approved work. If the mechanic won't write up a work order, DON'T LET HIM OR HER WORK ON YOUR CAR.

1.109 Ask for the Replaced Parts Back. This can be valuable evidence of what work was actually done. You must ask for these BEFORE work is done on your car to be sure of getting the parts. Keep them for awhile to be sure the repair is okay. It is best to put this request in writing on the work order.

A few parts are always returned to the maker and so will not be returned to you.

1.110 New or Used Parts. To save money, it is sometimes possible to use a rebuilt or a used part rather than a new one. Be sure you and the mechanic are clear on which is to be installed. Rebuilt parts almost always have a warranty or guarantee for a set period of time. Used parts may or may not have this protection. All warranties or guarantees must be in writing.

1.111 Don't Leave Property in the Car. Most garages have signs posted saying the garage is not responsible for items left in the car. This is correct. If you must leave the car overnight, find out where the car will be kept. The mechanic is responsible for damage or theft only if he or she is negligent in some fashion.

True Story Number Six

Joe's car needs repair. He takes it in for repair. He sees the sign that says the owner is not responsible for articles left in the car. Joe carefully removes his baseball equipment, school books, coat, and anything else that was loose in the car. He must leave the car several days.

When he goes to pick it up, he discovers that someone has ripped the in-dash tape player out. This is an old car, and Joe does not carry vandalism insurance on it. He goes to the garage owner. After all, the car was in the owner's custody. The owner refuses to pay for the damage and points to the sign about articles left in the car. Joe looks at him in disbelief.

"This wasn't 'left' in the car. It was part of the car," Joe says. The garage owner just shrugs.

Joe sues the garage owner in small claims court (see § 7.4). He wins but never collects his money before the garage owner files for bankruptcy.

None of this was really Joe's fault. This time he could not have avoided the problem. Chalk it up to the first of my rules to live by: "Life is not fair."

1.112 *Warranties.* This is a guarantee of *free* replacement or repair for a set period of time. Warranties can be on many different things. Some examples are:

1. *New car warranty:* For a set number of miles or specific period of time (see § 1.91 on new car purchases for more details).

2. *Extended warranty:* This is an optional feature that you can buy when you buy a new car. Extended warranties vary greatly in length, cost, and coverage.

3. *Parts warranty:* New parts and rebuilt parts usually have a warranty for a set period of time.

4. *Warranty of labor:* The mechanic may warrant or guarantee his work (parts and labor) for a set period of time.

SPECIAL NOTE: Get all warranties in WRITING. A verbal guarantee is next to impossible to prove.

1.113 *Save All Paperwork.* It is vital to have all receipts, work orders, estimates, and warranties for proof if you later need to question what was done or not done.

1.114 *Unauthorized Work.* Upon arrival to pick up your car, you discover that work you DID NOT authorize was done. The mechanic failed to call you. TECHNICALLY, you don't have to pay for the extra work, BUT the mechanic can remove whatever parts were used in the unauthorized work and put your old ones back on. In other words, he or she doesn't get to benefit from unauthorized work, BUT *neither do you.* Often it is impractical or impossible to have the mechanic undo the work. You may have to pay under protest and follow the steps in §§ 1.116–1.122.

1.115 *Higher Charges.* You authorized all of the work, but the cost is higher than you were told. If you have "binding estimate" noted in writing, you have the law on your side. Keep calm and try to reason with the mechanic. Most cases of higher charges occur on estimates that were not binding. If binding is not written on the estimate, you may have to pay.

1.116 *What Can You Do?* Stay calm and polite. It is very difficult to get people to do what you want if you are screaming at them. The mechanic's instinctive response is to scream back and stick to his or her guns. Calmness and politeness should correct the problem if it is simply an error. If the mechanic says it is no error and reasoning with him or her fails, go over his or her head to an owner or manager. If this fails, READ ON.

1.117 *Pay under Protest.* If you want your car back, you will have to pay to get your car. A MECHANIC'S LIEN allows the mechanic to hold the car until you pay. You may note in the memo area on your check the words "under protest."

1.118 *Do Not Stop Payment on the Check.* In some circumstances, this is a *crime.* You don't want to wake up to sheriff's deputies on your doorstep at 6:00 A.M. with a warrant for your ARREST! In some circumstances it isn't a crime, BUT this is a technical point. You'd need a lawyer to figure out the difference. It is not worth the risk of going to jail.

1.119 *Mechanics Lien.* Not only can the mechanic hold your car until you pay, *but* if he or she releases the car to you and your check bounces, is returned because payment is stopped, or the account is closed, HE OR SHE CAN RETAKE YOUR CAR. He or she can't take it out of a locked garage, but he or she can take it from almost any place else. This doesn't happen very often, but it can happen. The mechanic can hold it until you pay.

1.120 *Complain to Better Business Bureau or the Attorney General's Office.* These agencies require a written statement setting forth the problem with the mechanic in full detail. Once filed, these agencies contact the mechanic for a response. They will attempt to negotiate an acceptable settlement of the issue. They both work in the spirit of cooperation. Neither agency can *force* the mechanic to do what you want, but they are frequently successful anyway. Filing is free. You may file with either one or both agencies. The BBB is listed in the business pages of your phone book. The attorney general's offices are listed in this book in § 7.2. Contact the one nearest you.

1.121 *Dispute Resolution Center.* See § 7.3 for more information. This service may be able to resolve your problem.

1.122 *File Suit.* You can do this yourself in small claims court for amounts up to $5,000. A lawyer is not required. For a higher amount you must go to a higher court with a lawyer.

You may be able to sue under the *Deceptive Trade Practices Act* for three times the amount, in certain cases. For this kind of suit you need a lawyer.

1.123 *Dissatisfaction with the Work.* If the problem comes back, take the car back. The mechanic should fix it (if it is a new car under warranty, see LEMON LAW in § 1.92). If the same problem occurs again, you may want to take the car to another mechanic for an opinion. If you suspect work was not done that you were charged for, take the car to another mechanic with the work order and re-turned parts. He or she may be able to tell you if work was done at all OR if work was improperly done.

Get the second mechanic's opinion in writing. Go back to the first mechanic and attempt to reason with him or her. If this doesn't work, follow all of the steps noted above for DISPUTED BILLS.

How many times must you allow the first mechanic to repair the same problem? Probably several. If it is still not fixed, take the car to a second mechanic.

You can try to insist that the first mechanic PAY for the second mechanic to fix the problem, but it may not work. In that case you must just pay the second mechanic yourself and sue the first one.

1.124 *Leaving the Car with the Mechanic.* Whether you leave it because you don't have the money to pay an undisputed bill or you leave it because you are disputing the bill, DON'T leave it for several months. The mechanic can charge you reasonable storage fees at a daily rate. When the bill plus storage fees equals the value of the car, THE MECHANIC CAN SELL THE CAR.

1.125 *Lemon Law.*   See § 1.92.

Chapter 2
Pranks and Other Crimes

You will see many things done on television or in the movies that are shown as fun pranks. Nobody ever gets into any real trouble from doing them. It is all presented as a big joke. Well, that is the movies or TV, not real life.

In real life, many of those "fun pranks" are CRIMES. Crimes lead to punishment that few people find funny. KNOW BEFORE YOU ACT, and avoid nasty surprises.

The Truth about Arrest and Jail

2.1 *Being Read Your Rights.* On TV, as the officer fastens the handcuffs, he or she reads you your "rights." *In real life, it doesn't happen that way.*

Your "rights," called the Miranda warning, state that you don't have to answer questions, that you have the right to talk to an attorney before questioning, and that an attorney will be appointed for you if you can't afford one.

If the officer arresting you is not planning to get a confession from you, he or she doesn't have to read you your rights. If the officer DOES get a confession to the crime, without having read you your rights, *the confession* is *probably invalid,* but not the arrest. FAILURE TO READ YOU YOUR RIGHTS NEVER INVALIDATES THE ARREST.

2.2 *You Are an Adult at Age 17 If You Commit a Crime.* For the purpose of committing a crime, you are treated as an adult at age 17. That means you can be given the full punishment allowed by law. For every other purpose, except drinking alcohol, you are treated as an adult at age 18. As you know, to buy and drink alcohol legally, you must be 21 or in the company of your parents or your 21-year-old or older spouse.

2.3 *What Really Happens If You Are Arrested and Jailed.* Whether you are arrested on traffic-ticket warrants or for murder, the process is basically the same.

1. *Handcuffs:* Most officers use them on ALL offenders, even women, regardless of the reason for the arrest. They are used for the officer's protection. They are frequently fastened tight enough to leave marks on your wrists when they are removed. That is *not* illegal.

2. *Treatment:* People complain, "I was treated like a criminal." Once arrested, regardless of what the arrest was for, in the eyes of the officers and jailors, you are a criminal. They may not be polite, and your handling may not be gentle.

3. *Mug shots and fingerprints:* These are taken of all people jailed, regardless of the charge.

4. *Searches:* I mean searches of your person. The officer who initially stops you can do a pat-down search of you for weapons. At the jail, a thorough search of you is done before you are put in a cell.

5. *Holding cells:* Jails don't have a special cell for traffic offenders, college students, or young people. If you are 17 or older, you're put in the holding cell with whomever else has been recently arrested. On TV, the holding cell is never crowded, and the other prisoners are asleep or friendly. In reality, most jails are crowded, there are no empty bunks, and your fellow prisoners are not pleasant to smell or talk to.

6. *Phone call:* You have the legal right to one phone call. You'll make it at the jailor's convenience, not yours. You may get to make it right away, or it may be hours later. Use this call to arrange bail money to get out of jail.

7. *Length of detention after bond is made or fine paid:* This can be a long time. The courts have allowed at least 24 hours. You're released at the jail's convenience, not yours. If you are waiting to go before a judge, it can be longer.

SPECIAL NOTE: If you are arrested for driving while intoxicated (DWI), you will be held at least four hours, regardless of when bail is posted.

True Story Number Seven

Remember True Story Number Two when Joe got arrested for cursing the officer? After he bonded out of jail, Joe went to see his attorney.

After telling his version of what happened, Joe wails, "You won't believe where they put me. I thought jails were segregated."

His lawyer blinks and thinks, "Hasn't this guy ever heard of the Civil Rights movement? Surely he doesn't mean racially segregated."

The lawyer asks Joe, "Do you mean racially segregated?"

Joe says, "No, no, no. Not that. I mean they put me in with the criminals."

Puzzled, the lawyer says, "Where did you expect them to put you?"

Joe says, "Don't they have a separate cell for college students?"

The lawyer nearly dies laughing.

No, there is no separate cell for young people over 16 years of age, for traffic offenders, or for college students. You get thrown in the tank with anyone else recently arrested.

2.4 *How to Get Out of Jail.* You can get out of jail by paying a fine or posting bond.

1. *Pay the fine:* If you want to plead guilty and pay the fine, the judge will be contacted to set the amount of the fine. You may have to wait to be taken in front of the judge for him or her to set the fine in person.

Once the fine is set, you can pay the money or "lay the fine out in jail." How much of the fine you are credited with per day varies from county to county. Most people do this only if the offense is a Class C misdemeanor.

If in doubt whether this is the correct thing to do in your case, DON'T DO IT. Once you've done it, it can't be undone. IF IN DOUBT, BOND OUT.

2. *Post bond:* A bond is a guarantee or promise that you won't skip town and ignore your trial date. The different types of bond include:

a) *Personal recognizance bond (PR bond):* You sign a paper bond in which you promise to appear for all court appearances when so ordered. The guarantee that you'll appear is your promise. A judge must approve this bond. If your offense is not serious and people know you and affirm your reliability, then you may get one. If you fail to appear when you are supposed to, a warrant is issued for your arrest, and you owe the amount of the bond to the state.

b) *Cash bond:* If the bond is set at $1,000, you can pay $1,000 cash to the sheriff's escrow account to guarantee you'll appear for all court appearances. If you fail to appear, the money is forfeited, and a warrant for your arrest is issued. When you appear as ordered and your case is completed, YOU GET BACK THE CASH IN FULL, but without interest. This is the cheapest way to go, if you have the cash.

c) *Bond through an attorney: Some* attorneys will guarantee your promise to appear for all court appearances with a paper bond. The paper bond does not require you to pay cash for the bond amount, UNLESS you skip town. The attorney may charge a fee for this guarantee, over and above his or her regular legal fee. ONLY A FEW ATTORNEYS DO THIS and usually only if they already know you. If you do not appear, a warrant is issued for your arrest, and you owe the state the amount of the bond. You'll probably have to find a new attorney, too.

d) *Bail bond:* Most people use this because no PR bond was granted, they don't have enough cash to post as bond, and they don't know an attorney who makes bonds. You pay a *nonrefundable fee* to a professional bail bondsman to post a paper bond for the amount of the bond. The fee is less than the total amount of the bond. The bondsman guarantees to the court that you will show up for all court appearances. You avoid having to pay the full amount of the bond, as you do in a cash bond situation, *but you don't ever get any money back.* You also don't have to sit in jail. You will have to maintain close contact with the bondsman.

The amount of the fee varies from town to town and bondsman to bondsman. With only one phone call from jail, you can't shop around for the cheapest. You could use your phone call to notify a friend and ask him or her to shop around for the cheapest fee. If you *don't* show up in court when ordered to do so, you and the bondsman owe the court the full amount of the bond, and a warrant is issued for your arrest. The bondsman also starts looking for you. It is much harder and more expensive to find a bondsman a second time if you've violated your bond the first time.

2.5 *How Much Will the Bond Be?*   A judge sets the amount of the bond; therefore, the amounts vary from judge to judge and town to town. The seriousness of the crime is one factor in setting the amount of the bond.

Common misdemeanor offenses, such as DWI and public intoxication, have *preset* bonds. That means the judge has already set the amount of bond for all DWI's or public intoxication charges. Therefore, you don't have to appear before a judge to find out the amount of the bond.

On more unusual crimes and especially on felonies, the judge must be consulted. Usually this is done by taking you before a judge to enter a plea. This is your *arraignment*. If you want to bond out, *you must plead not guilty.* The judge will then set the amount of your bond. When you make bond in one of the ways described in § 2.4 above, you get out of jail.

What Happens in Court?

2.6 *Arraignment.*   This is your first appearance in court before a judge to enter a plea and have bond set, if it has not been done already.

If there was a preset bond on your offense, you will have bonded out BEFORE you see a judge (for more about bonds, see §§ 2.4 and 2.5).

If you need a court-appointed attorney, ask for him or her now (see § 2.10 for more information). A court date for your next appearance will be set.

2.7 *Entering a Plea.*   WHEN IN DOUBT, PLEAD NOT GUILTY. Your plea can always be changed later if you change your mind. Pleading not guilty allows your attorney maneuvering room to plea bargain or represent you in trial.

Pleading GUILTY or NO CONTEST means no plea bargaining. You may get a harsher punishment, and you may have to pay the fine or spend time in jail right away.

2.8 *Do You Need an Attorney?*   If you are charged with an offense that is a Class B misdemeanor or higher, YES.

If you are charged with a Class C misdemeanor, it depends. If you want to go to trial on the charge, you should have a lawyer. However, you are allowed by law to represent yourself if you choose to do so.

If you want to plead guilty and pay the fine, you don't necessarily need an attorney, BUT an attorney might be able to get you a smaller fine. You would, of course, have to pay the attorney's fees.

2.9 Finding an Attorney.   Ask family and friends for referrals. Your local bar association may have a referral service. The state bar association does have a referral service. Call 1–800–252–9690 and tell the operator which city or town you are in and that you need an attorney for criminal law.

You can shop for yourself by checking the phone book. Attorneys will be listed alphabetically in the yellow pages under "attorney." Some attorneys will have advertisements that indicate they practice criminal law.

Your best bet is to shop around and talk to several attorneys. Feeling comfortable with an attorney you choose is as important as the amount of the fee (for further information on choosing a lawyer, see §§ 7.6–7.10).

2.10 Court-Appointed Attorneys.   You can ask for a court-appointed attorney at your arraignment. You must satisfy the judge that you are too indigent (poor) to hire an attorney. If you can't afford to bond out of jail, then obviously you can't afford a lawyer. If you can afford to make bond, it is harder (but not impossible) to convince the judge that you are too poor to hire a lawyer. If you are supported by your parents while going to college but have no money yourself, it is difficult to convince a judge that he or she should appoint an attorney. The judge will have little sympathy with your desire not to tell your parents about your arrest.

An appointed attorney is ethically bound to do his or her best to represent you as well as a hired attorney would.

Some cities have a public defender office that represents you in these cases. In cities that don't, a private attorney will be appointed.

SPECIAL NOTE: Under Texas law you ARE NOT ENTITLED to a court-appointed attorney if you are charged with a Class C misdemeanor. If you want a trial and cannot afford to hire an attorney, you will have to represent yourself. Class C misdemeanors are the least serious crimes.

2.11 Plea Bargaining.   During the time between your arraignment and trial, your attorney will attempt to bargain with the prosecuting attorney to get you the best possible deal. If an acceptable bargain is reached, you will plead guilty in exchange for a specific punishment probation or deferred adjudication promised by the prosecuting attorney. This can work out best for everyone. You save money in attorney's fees by not going to trial, and you aren't gambling on what the punishment will be. The state disposes of a case without the cost and time for a trial.

2.12 *Trial.* If no acceptable plea bargain is reached, or you want to go to trial, then a trial date is set. It will usually be several months, sometimes a year, before the trial. The more serious the crime, the longer it takes to get to trial, as a general rule. You can change your mind and plead guilty any time.

If you go to trial, you should be represented by an attorney. Technically, you can represent yourself in any court, but it is not wise to do so. Trials are generally too complicated for the nonlawyer. The one exception to this general rule is, as stated above, on a Class C misdemeanor case. This trial is simpler, and if you lose, the maximum penalty is only a fine of $500.

If you want to represent yourself on a traffic ticket, see §§ 1.20–1.29.

2.13 *Appeals.* The appeals process almost always requires a lawyer.

Classification of Crimes and Their Punishment

Below are the classifications of most criminal offenses and the name of the court that would try the case. Refer back to this section to find out the punishment on a specific offense. See attached diagram for further court information.

2.14 *Justice Court or Municipal Court.*
Class C misdemeanor—up to $500 fine.

2.15 *County Court or County Court-at-Law.*
Class B misdemeanor—up to 6 months in jail and/or a fine of up to $2,000.
Class A misdemeanor—up to 12 months in jail and/or a fine up to $4,000.

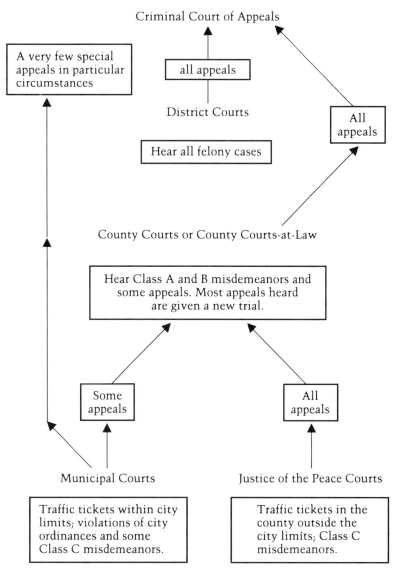

Remember, Most, If Not All Appeals, Require a Lawyer.

2.16 *District Court.*

State jail felony—6 months to 2 years in a state jail; in addition, a possible fine not to exceed $10,000.

Third-Degree felony—2 to 10 years in the penitentiary; in addition, a possible fine not to exceed $10,000.

Second-Degree felony—2 to 20 years in the penitentiary; in addition, a possible fine not to exceed $10,000.
First-Degree felony—life or 5 to 99 years in the penitentiary; in addition, a possible fine not to exceed $10,000.
Capital felony—life imprisonment or death by lethal injection.

2.17 Nonclassified Crimes. There are certain other criminal offenses that do not fall under these classifications. The punishment on these offenses will be noted when the offense is described.

Specific Crimes

The penal code and other statute books are filled with numerous crimes. Those listed below are some that are likely to be of most interest to you. It is not intended as a complete list. Remember, most of these crimes lead to an arrest and jail on the day of the arrest, as well as the statutory punishment. Drugs and alcohol-related crimes will be covered in separate sections at the end of this section.

If the punishment is not stated, refer to the punishments listed in §§ 2.14–2.16.

2.18 Hazing. Yes, hazing is a CRIME. Hazing consists of any intentional, knowing, or reckless act that endangers the mental or physical safety of a student, including, but not limited to:

1. Physical brutality.

2. Physical activity like sleep deprivation, exposure to weather, confinement in a small space, or calisthenics.

3. Requiring the eating or drinking of any substance that causes unreasonable risk of harm.

4. Any activity that intimidates, threatens, causes ostracism, extreme mental stress, shame, humiliation, or causes loss of dignity.

Punishment is for individuals and the organization.
If an individual engages in hazing, encourages, directs, or aids hazing, knowingly permits hazing to occur, or has firsthand knowledge of hazing and fails to report it to the college or university, he or she is guilty of hazing.

PUNISHMENT:

1. *Failure to report:*

Class B misdemeanor

2. *Everything else:*

a) NO SERIOUS BODILY INJURY—Class B misdemeanor

b) SERIOUS BODILY INJURY—Class A misdemeanor

c) DEATH—State jail felony

If the organization, an officer, or any combinations of members, pledges, or alumni CONDONE, ENCOURAGE, COMMIT, OR ASSIST in hazing, they can be found guilty.

PUNISHMENT:

1. *No property damage or physical injury:* Fine of not less than $5,000 nor more than $10,000.

2. *Personal injury, property damage, or death:* Fine of not less than $5,000 nor more than double the amount lost or expenses incurred.

Remember, CONSENT to hazing is NEVER a defense. IMMUNITY from prosecution is available to those testifying for the prosecution. Nothing prevents the college or university from imposing its own punishment against the organization and individual members. In addition, if physical injury or death occurs, civil lawsuits are likely to be filed against the organization and its members. Don't be fooled into thinking that a prosecutor has more serious crimes to prosecute than hazing. In the recent past both females and males have been prosecuted.

2.19 *Theft.* This offense covers a lot of ground. It includes shoplifting, stealing street signs, stealing firewood out of someone's yard, stealing hanging plants off someone's porch, taking dairy crates and shopping carts and items left in or around a Goodwill drop box, or taking *and keeping* the class ring you found left in the restroom at school, or stealing a car.

How serious the theft is depends on the value of the item taken.
Under $50—Class C misdemeanor
$50 up to $500—Class B misdemeanor
$500 up to $1,500—Class A misdemeanor
$1,500 up to $20,000—State jail felony
$20,000 up to $100,000—Third-Degree felony

Very seldom will an offer to return the item or pay for it result in charges being dropped.

SPECIAL NOTE: For future employment chances, THEFT is one of the worst things to have on your record. A prospective employer is not going to believe that it was a joke or a prank. He or she will think you are dishonest, not trustworthy, and not someone he or she wants to hire.

I strongly recommend that you hire an attorney to represent you if you are charged with theft at any level.

True Story Number Eight

Joe Anyone and his roommate Clyde go to the grocery store to get provisions for their apartment. Since they are completely out of food, they are both hungry. Passing the potato chip aisle, they grab a 35-cent package of potato chips (you know, the size your mom put in your lunch when you were a kid). They open the potato chips and eat them while shopping.

By the time Joe and Clyde reach the check-out counter, the chip bag is empty. They fully intend to pay for the chips, but the check-out clerk ignores the empty sack left in the basket. Joe and Clyde, paying no attention, don't mention it. They pay for $50 worth of groceries but do not pay the 35 cents for the chips.

They pick up the grocery sacks and leave the store. Once outside, they hear, "Freeze, you're under arrest." All the store security guards appear and escort Joe and Clyde back into the store. Joe and Clyde are accused of stealing the chips. They apologize and offer to pay, saying that it is all a mistake. Their offer is refused.

The police are called. Joe and Clyde figure that when the police arrive, the whole thing will get straightened out. Surely no officer is going to take two people to jail for a theft of 35 cents!

Wrong! The officers arrive, handcuff Joe and Clyde, and lead them through the store. They are booked and jailed.

By this time, Joe knows what to do: Plead not guilty, bond out, and hire a lawyer. Maybe the lawyer can get the city attorney to dismiss charges. If not, Joe can go to a jury trial on a theft of 35 cents!

2.20 *Hot Checks.* Everyone messes up once in awhile and accidentally gives a hot check. As long as you promptly take care of the check with the merchant, there is no problem. If you don't, it can become serious very quickly.

By law, the merchant must notify you at the address on the check by certified mail that you have given him or her a hot check. Certified mail must be hand delivered to a person at the address who signs a receipt. If no one is home, the postman leaves a notice, telling you to come to the post office to pick up the letter. DO IT! If you fail to pick up the certified letter, it is sent back to the merchant. The merchant can then proceed as though you had gotten the letter BUT ignored it. The letter must give you 10 days to pay for the check. If you fail to do so or fail to pick up the letter, the merchant can take the letter and the check to the district or county attorney to FILE CRIMINAL HOT-CHECK CHARGES against you. Not only will you have to pay the check, but also you can be arrested, have to pay a large fine, and end up with a CRIMINAL RECORD.

Some merchants use a check collection company BEFORE they send the certified letter. These companies call or write you. If you fail to pay the check with fees by whatever time limit they set, your name goes on a list. Any merchant who uses their service will refuse to accept your check for as long as it stays on the list. This is very inconvenient, to say the least.

SPECIAL NOTE: CHECK COLLECTION OR SERVICE FEES. Yes, it is legal to charge you a service fee if you give a hot check. $25 is the maximum charge.

2.21 *Account-Closed Checks.* These can be treated just like a hot check *or worse.* Most merchants will send you a certified letter, BUT THEY ARE NOT REQUIRED TO DO SO. The merchant can file criminal charges without the certified letter. You are presumed to know when you close the account, so you need no notification by mail.

2.22 *Penalties on Hot Checks and Account-Closed Checks.* Any check can be filed as a Class C misdemeanor under the worthless check statute, or it can be filed as a theft and classified by its amount.

Up to $20—Class C misdemeanor
$20 up to $500—Class B misdemeanor
$500 up to $1,500—Class A misdemeanor
$1,500 up to $20,000—State jail felony

True Story Number Nine

Joe and Sam Anyone have a sister named Susie. She has just returned to her own apartment for the fall semester. During the summer, she lived at home in another city. At 6:00 A.M. someone pounds on her door. Barely awake, she answers the door. Two sheriff's deputies are on the porch with a warrant for her arrest.

Shocked awake, she asks what the warrant is for. They tell her it is for a $1.98 check she gave last spring, when she was living in the dorm. She closed her account for the summer and failed to leave enough in the account to cover the check. The check was returned to the merchant, unpaid and stamped account closed.

She did not have her mail forwarded for the summer and therefore got no notices. Now it is too late for notices. A warrant has been issued. She owes the $1.98 plus $150 in fines and court costs.

The deputies tell her to get dressed and bring her purse. They can't take her before the judge before 8:00 A.M., so she will have to wait in jail. She begins to cry. She doesn't have any cash, and the judge won't take a check. She begs the deputies to let her call her big brother, Joe. He can lend her the money. They say okay. She calls Joe at home, but he's not there. She gets dressed and calls him again, hoping that he was in the shower before. Still no answer.

She begs the deputies not to arrest her. The tears work. The deputies say she can take herself before the judge at 9:00 A.M. with the money. That way she can avoid jail. If she fails to show, they'll be back.

Joe finally gets out of the shower and answers her third call. Fortunately, he has just cashed his check from home the day before and hasn't had a chance to spend it. He goes with her to court at 9:00 A.M., pays $200, and Susie avoids going to jail.

Remember, this was over a $1.98 check!

SPECIAL NOTE TO ALL SUSIE ANYONES: Tears may work on male officers but seldom on female officers.

2.23 *Chain Letters.* Once and for all, CHAIN LETTERS ARE NOT LEGAL. Even if the letter tells you it does not violate U.S. postal laws or Texas laws, *it usually does.* If the only way you make money is by introducing a new person to the scheme, IT IS ILLEGAL. It is illegal to set up such a scheme. The offense is a Class B misdemeanor.

2.24 *Vandalism.* The statute calls it "criminal mischief," and it means defacing, damaging, or destroying the property of another. The punishment is set by the value of the item destroyed or the amount of damage done. It is the same scale noted in § 2.22 for hot checks.

2.25 *Abusive, Indecent, Profane, or Vulgar Language or Gestures.* Use of this type of language or gesture in a public place is illegal. Your car has been ruled a "public place" if you're on a public street or highway. This means telling or showing the officer what you think of him or her after he or she gives you a ticket CAN LAND YOU IN JAIL. Think whatever you want, but BE POLITE. It isn't worth going to jail over. This is a disorderly conduct offense and is a Class C misdemeanor.

2.26 *Too Much Noise.* Making unreasonable noise in a public place OR near a private residence you do not occupy is a crime under the disorderly conduct statute. If the music is too loud at your party, the officers can arrest you. As the host of the party, you are responsible for the actions and noise of your guests. Usually, you'll get a warning to lower the noise level, but NO WARNING IS REQUIRED. This is a Class C misdemeanor.

2.27 *Mooning or Taking a Leak Outside.* Exposing yourself, front or rear, in public, and being reckless about whether you are offending or alarming anyone is a CRIME. It is disorderly conduct and a Class B misdemeanor.

2.28 *Telephone Harassment, Including Misuse of 911.* You commit an offense if you telephone someone with intent to harass, annoy, alarm, abuse, torment, or embarrass in any of the following ways:

1. You make a comment, suggestion, or proposal that is obscene.

2. You threaten to inflict serious bodily injury or commit a felony against the person you are talking to or a member of his or her family or his or her property.

3. You falsely report that someone has been injured or killed, knowing that it's false.

4. You cause the telephone to ring repeatedly or call anonymously.

5. You intentionally fail to hang up or disconnect.

6. You knowingly permit your phone to be used as listed above.

These are all Class B misdemeanors.

It is also an offense to call 911 when there is no emergency. It is an offense to call 911 and knowingly remain silent or abuse or harass the 911 employee. It is also an offense to allow your phone to be used in this manner. The first offense is a Class B misdemeanor.

SPECIAL NOTE: Emergency 911 systems automatically trace *all* calls back to a phone number and address, so it is easy to catch the caller.

2.29 *Bomb Threats and False Reports to Police or Fire Department.* In addition to the 911 statute, there is a separate law that deals with bomb threats and false reports of crimes or emergencies. These are Class A misdemeanors.

2.30 *Trespassing.* If you had notice that entry was forbidden either by being told or by posted signs or the presence of an obvious enclosure intended to keep out intruders (like a fence), it is a crime to go onto the property. If it is not a house, it is a Class B misdemeanor. Trespassing at a house or apartment is a Class A misdemeanor. Climbing the fence around the football stadium at night as a prank is a CRIME, even if you damage nothing. Climbing a TV or radio tower is also trespassing.

2.31 *Evading Arrest.* It is a CRIME to intentionally flee from a police officer who is attempting to arrest or detain you. This is a Class B misdemeanor, unless you flee in a car, which is a Class A misdemeanor.

2.32 *Resisting Arrest or Search.* This is a Class A misdemeanor unless a deadly weapon is used—then it is a Third-Degree felony.

2.33 *Failure to Identify.* It is illegal to intentionally refuse to give your name, address, or date of birth to the officers who have lawfully arrested you. It is also illegal to give a false name, address, or date of birth, if the officer believes you to be a witness to a crime. This is a Class C misdemeanor.

2.34 *Hindering Apprehension or Arrest.* If you hide, provide aid, or warn someone that officers are seeking to arrest him or her, it is a Class A misdemeanor, unless the person you aid is charged with a felony—then your crime becomes a felony, too.

2.35 *Assault.* Assault comes in various categories. You have committed an assault if you intentionally or knowingly threaten someone with imminent bodily injury or cause physical contact that you should know is offensive, like a shove. These are Class C misdemeanors, unless committed against an elderly or disabled individual. Then the crime becomes a Class A misdemeanor.

If you intentionally and knowingly cause bodily injury to someone in an assault, it is a Class A misdemeanor, unless it is against a public servant in lawful discharge of an official duty, in which case it is a Third-Degree felony.

If you intentionally and knowingly assault someone causing *serious* bodily injury, or *use a deadly weapon,* this charge is a Second-Degree felony, unless the person assaulted is a public servant lawfully discharging his or her public duty, or the assault is in retaliation against a witness, prospective witness, or informant of a crime, then it is a First-Degree felony.

An assault is defined as an *unprovoked attack.*

SPECIAL NOTE: In Texas, words are NEVER legal provocation for an assault. If someone refers in a negative fashion to your ancestry, you CANNOT respond by hitting that person without committing an assault.

2.36 *Statutory Rape.* If you have sex or oral sex with a person not your spouse, who is younger than 17, it is a Second-Degree felony. If the child is under 14, it can be filed as a First-Degree felony. If you are not more than three years older than the victim, it is also a defense to prosecution. The *bottom line* is that sex with someone under 17 is very RISKY, because that person cannot give legal consent. Parents can file charges, even if the person you had sex with doesn't want to file charges.

2.37 *Rape.* The bottom line is that either partner has the absolute RIGHT to say NO, no matter what has been said or done earlier.

Provocative manner or clothing doesn't matter. It doesn't matter how many times you've done it together before. If the other partner says NO and you do it anyway, you can be charged with RAPE. It is a Second-Degree felony, unless a weapon, threat, or force is used. Then it is a First-Degree felony.

2.38 *Unauthorized Use of a Vehicle.* Operating a car, truck, boat, or airplane *without the owner's permission* used to be called "joy riding." You have "borrowed" the vehicle with full intent to return it, rather than having stolen it with no intent to return. However, this is a State jail felony. For car theft, see § 2.19.

2.39 *Walking a Restaurant or Motel Tab.*   Leaving without paying your bill is theft of service. The seriousness of the charge depends on the amount of the tab.

Up to $20—Class C misdemeanor
$20 up to $500—Class B misdemeanor
$500 up to $1,500—Class A misdemeanor
$1,500 and up—State jail felony

2.40 *Video Tapes.*   If you fail to return video tapes or a VCR or other rental property on the due date, the owner must send you a notice by certified mail, demanding return of the property. If you fail to return it within 10 days of the notice, you are presumed to have STOLEN the property. Criminal theft charges will be filed. The seriousness of the offense depends on how much money is involved (see § 2.39 above for the punishment; see § 6.15 for *civil* penalties).

2.41 *Burglary of a Building.*   Entering a habitation or a building not then open to the public or remaining inside a building after closing hours with intent to commit a felony or theft is burglary. Burglary of a habitation (house, apartment, mobile home, etc.) is a Second-Degree felony. Burglary of any other building is a State jail felony. If the burglar intends to or attempts to commit a felony other than theft, then it becomes a First-Degree felony.

SPECIAL NOTE: Notice that this statute DOES NOT require "breaking and entering." You don't have to "break" in. If you go in through the unlocked front door, you have committed a burglary. Also, just the INTENT to commit a felony or theft is enough to convict you. You don't have to have actually committed the felony or theft.

True Story Number Ten

Sam Anyone left his studies on a Wednesday night to visit a bar. Even though Sam is under 21, he drinks enough liquor to be feeling no pain. Sam and his friends leave the bar together on foot to walk home. They pass a convenience store that is obviously closed because it is dark. As they pass the rear of the store, they see the store's back door standing wide open. Someone has obviously broken in, although there is no one around.

Sam's friends have also drunk enough so that their judgment has been affected.

Instead of calling the officers or just leaving the scene, they dare Sam to go in the store to steal a candy bar. Sam accepts the dare and goes inside. A police car arrives on the scene. Sam's "friends" run away, leaving Sam in the building. He is caught inside. Sam tries to explain to the officers about the dare, but the officers arrest Sam for BURGLARY.

Sam uses his one phone call to call big brother, Joe. Joe, now an expert on making bond, gets Sam out of jail. Sam has to hire a lawyer and hope that the lawyer can convince the district attorney that Sam DID NOT burglarize the store. If he is lucky, the charge will be reduced to theft of the candy bar. The testimony of his friends will be critical.

2.42 *Burglary of Coin-Operated Machines.* If you break in or enter the machine in some other way, with intent to obtain money or goods, you have committed burglary of a coin-operated machine. This is a Class A misdemeanor. Coin-operated machines include pay telephones.

2.43 *Burglary of a Vehicle.* Breaking into or entering into a vehicle or any part of a vehicle with intent to commit a felony or theft is burglary of a vehicle and punishable as a Class A misdemeanor.

2.44 *Credit or Debit Card Abuse.* It is a State jail felony to steal a credit or debit card, use or attempt to use a stolen card or a card number not your own, or to sell or buy a credit or debit card. It is also a State jail felony to obtain property or service or attempt to obtain property or service with a *fictitious* credit card. It is also a State jail felony to use a credit card knowing that it is expired, canceled, or revoked.

2.45 *Forgery.* If the writing you have forged is a will, codicil, deed of trust, mortgage, security instrument, security agreement, *credit card*, or *check*, it is a State jail felony. It is a Third-Degree felony if the forged item is money, securities, postage, revenue stamps, or other instrument issued by a state or national government (including *driver's license* or DPS-issued *identification card*; for further information on this, see §§ 1.80 and 1.81). Under this statute it is illegal to possess with intent to use, to attempt to use, or to make a forged item.

2.46 *False Statement to Obtain Property or Credit.*   It is a Class A misdemeanor to make a materially false or misleading written statement to obtain property or credit.

2.47 *Unauthorized Use of Television or Cable Descrambling, Decoding, or Interception Device.*   It is a Class B misdemeanor to *use* such a device. It is a Class A misdemeanor if you were paid by someone else to set this up for them to use.

2.48 *Tampering with Manufacturer's Identification Number.*   It is a Class A misdemeanor to knowingly remove, alter, or wipe out a manufacturer's permanent identification number on personal property, such as TV's, VCR's, cameras, stereos, bicycles, guns, and so forth.

Weapons

Certain weapons are always illegal to carry or possess. Other weapons are legal to possess only in certain circumstances.

2.49 *Illegal Weapons.*   It is *never* legal to possess, manufacture, transport, repair, or sell the following weapons:

1. An explosive weapon (bomb, grenade, rocket, or mine).

2. Machine gun.

3. Short-barrel firearm (rifle barrel shorter than 16 inches or shotgun barrel less than 18 inches, or overall length less than 26 inches).

4. Firearm silencer.

5. Switchblade knife.

6. Knuckles.

7. Armor-piercing ammunition.

8. A chemical dispensing device.

9. A zipgun.

Except for (5) and (6) above, this offense is a Third-Degree felony; (5) and (6) are Class A misdemeanors.

2.50 *Legal Weapons with Restrictions.* It is illegal to carry on your person a handgun, illegal knife, or club. This is a Class A misdemeanor.

1. A *handgun* is just what you think it is.

2. An *illegal knife* is:

   a) A knife with a blade longer than 5 1/2 inches.

   b) A hand instrument designed to cut or stab by being thrown (this appears to cover *martial arts throwing stars*).

   c) A dagger (including dirk, stiletto, and poniard).

   d) A bowie knife.

   e) A sword.

   f) A spear.

3. A *club* is an instrument specially adapted or designed for the purpose of inflicting serious bodily injury or death and includes (but is not limited to):

   a) A blackjack.

   b) A nightstick.

   c) A tomahawk.

   d) Numchucks (if you are using them for martial arts practice, keep them in the trunk of your car when not at the practice place or home and you should be okay; DO NOT KEEP THEM under the seat of the car or carry them with you outside your home or practice place. This isn't Japan, and you're not a Ninja warrior).

2.51 *When You May Possess Weapons.* You may possess a handgun, illegal knife, or club at your home, your place of business, or while traveling (more than across town), or if you are licensed in law enforcement, private security work, or private investigation.

If you are 21 years of age and have obtained a license to carry a concealed handgun, you may carry a concealed handgun on your person except where prohibited by § 2.52 or barred by posted notice.

2.52 *Places Where Weapons are Prohibited.* Taking a firearm, an explosive weapon, an illegal knife, or any weapon noted in

§ 2.49, to the following places is always illegal (even if you have a concealed handgun license):

1. The premises of a school or educational institution, public or private, unless the school permits it with written regulations.

2. The premises of a polling place on the day of an election.

3. Any court or office used by the court unless you have written authorization.

4. The premises of a racetrack or secured area of an airport.

5. It is also illegal to take a handgun, illegal knife, or club on premises licensed to sell *alcoholic beverages.*

Offenses under this section are Third-Degree felonies.

2.53 *Illegally Loaning Weapons.* It is illegal to:

1. Loan, sell, rent, or give a handgun to someone who intends to use it illegally.

2. Sell, rent, give, or offer to sell to any child under 18 a firearm, club, or illegal knife or any martial arts throwing stars without parent's permission.

3. Sell a firearm or ammunition to an intoxicated person.

These offenses are Class A misdemeanors.

Drugs

This is a listing of the most commonly used drugs. Possession is without a prescription, of course.

2.54 *Marijuana.* *Possession* of marijuana is punished according to how much you possessed, as follows:

1. A useable amount to 2 ounces—Class B misdemeanor.

2. More than 2 ounces to 4 ounces—Class A misdemeanor.

3. More than 4 ounces up to 5 pounds—State jail felony.

4. More than 5 pounds up to 50 pounds—Third-Degree felony.

5. More than 50 pounds to 2,000 pounds—Second-Degree felony.

6. More than 2,000 pounds—5 to 99 years or life and a fine not to exceed $50,000.

Delivery of marijuana is punished according to how much you delivered and to whom you delivered it, as follows:

1. One-quarter ounce or less for no money—Class B misdemeanor.

2. One-quarter ounce or less for money—Class A misdemeanor.

3. More than 1/4 ounce but no more than 5 pounds—State jail felony.

4. More than 5 pounds but no more than 50 pounds—Second-Degree felony.

5. More than 50 pounds but no more than 2,000 pounds—First-Degree felony.

6. More than 2,000 pounds—10 to 99 years or life and a fine not to exceed $100,000.

Delivery of marijuana or other drugs to someone *17 years of age or younger,* or to a student enrolled in elementary or secondary school, or to someone you believe will deliver it to one of the above is a Second-Degree felony.

2.55 *Cocaine.* This includes all types and derivatives, including, but not limited to, crack and crank.

Possession:

1. Less than 1 gram—State jail felony.

2. 1 gram but less than 4 grams—Third-Degree felony.

3. 4 grams but less than 200 grams—Second-Degree felony.

4. 200 grams but less than 400 grams—First-Degree felony.

5. 400 grams or more—10 to 99 years or life and a fine not to exceed $100,000.

Delivery, possession with intent to deliver, or manufacture:

1. Less than 1 gram—State jail felony.

2. 1 gram but less than 4 grams—Second-Degree felony.

3. 4 grams but less than 200 grams—First-Degree felony.

4. 200 grams but less than 400 grams—10 to 99 years or life and a fine not to exceed $100,000.

5. 400 grams or more—15 to 99 years or life and a fine not to exceed $250,000.

2.56 Amphetamines.   Also known as speed or uppers.
Possession:

1. Less than 1 gram—State jail felony.

2. 1 gram but less than 4 grams—Third-Degree felony.

3. 4 grams but less than 400 grams—Second-Degree felony.

4. 400 grams or more—5 to 99 years or life and a fine not to exceed $50,000.

Delivery, manufacture, possession with intent to manufacture or deliver:

1. Less than 1 gram—State jail felony.

2. 1 gram but less than 4 grams—Second-Degree felony.

3. 4 grams but less than 400 grams—First-Degree felony.

4. 400 grams or more—10 to 99 years or life and a fine not to exceed $100,000.

2.57 Methamphetamines (ice or ecstacy).   Same as cocaine, § 2.55.

2.58 Barbiturates.   Most barbiturates, also known as *downers,* are treated as follows:
Possession:

1. Less than 28 grams—Class A misdemeanor.

2. 28 grams but less than 200 grams—Third-Degree felony.

3. 200 grams but less than 400 grams—Second-Degree felony.

4. 400 grams or more—5 to 99 years or life and a fine not to exceed $50,000.

Delivery, manufacture, or possession with intent to manufacture or deliver:

1. Less than 28 grams—State jail felony.

2. 28 grams but less than 200 grams—Second-Degree felony.

3. 200 grams but less than 400 grams—First-Degree felony.

4. 400 grams or more—10 to 99 years or life and a fine not to exceed $100,000.

2.59 *Steroids.* Same as barbiturates, § 2.58.

2.60 *Heroin and Morphine.* Same as cocaine, § 2.55.

2.61 *Drug Paraphernalia.* *Possession for own use:* Class C misdemeanor.
Possession with intent to deliver:
First offense—Class A misdemeanor.
Second offense—90 days to 1 year in jail.

Sale by a person 18 years of age or older to a person less than 18 years of age and at least 3 years younger than the actor—State jail felony.

Alcohol-Related Offenses

The consumption of alcoholic beverages plays a large role in involving people with the criminal justice system. Generally, it is the consumption of too much alcohol that causes problems, but some offenses concern the age of the drinker.

For purposes of this section only, you are a "minor" if you are not yet 21 years of age.

SPECIAL NOTE: If you are convicted of purchase, consumption, or possession of alcoholic beverages as a minor, in addition to the punishment noted in the specific sections below, the judge *must* order you to attend an alcohol awareness course approved by the Texas Commission on Alcohol and Drug Abuse. Failure to attend this course within 90 days will result in suspension of your driver's license for up to 6 months.

2.62 *Minor in Possession (MIP).* If you are under 21 years of age, it is illegal to possess, consume, or purchase alcoholic beverages, unless you are in the company of your parents or your spouse who is 21 or older. Note that consumption (drinking it) is *not* required.

Frequently, the officer will issue a ticket for MIP, but he or she always has the right to arrest instead.

MIP is punishable by a fine of $25–$200 for the first offense and a fine of $500–$1,000 for subsequent offenses.

If you receive only one MIP conviction before you turn 21, you can have it erased from your record by contacting the judge of the court where you were convicted. You will have to sign a sworn statement that you have received no other convictions. If you get more than one conviction, all convictions will remain on your record.

True Story Number Eleven

To be sure Sam doesn't get in any more trouble, Joe keeps an eye on him. Joe decides to buy some beer at a convenience store. He is 21, so he can legally do so. Sam stays in the car (remember, Sam is not yet 21). Joe puts the beer in the back seat. He does *not* open one, because he knows it is illegal to drink and drive.

Unbeknownst to the Anyone brothers, they are being watched by police officers. The officers decide Sam is a minor, and they stop the car. The officers ticket Sam for minor in possession, even though Sam is in the front seat and the beer is in the back seat. They also ticket Joe for providing alcohol to a minor.

Joe can't believe it! Back to his lawyer once again. (This lawyer could make a career out of the Anyone family!) His lawyer has a good chance of proving that Sam did not possess alcohol nor did Joe give it to him, BUT it will probably have to be done in a trial. That means substantial attorney fees.

2.63 *Providing Alcoholic Beverages to a Minor.* This includes *purchasing* for a minor or *giving* it to a minor. You can commit this offense even if you are a minor yourself.

The punishment is a fine of $100–$500.

You may be ticketed for this offense or arrested at the officer's option. A parent or spouse, 21 or older, can legally give alcohol to a minor.

2.64 *Misrepresentation of Age by a Minor.* If you say you are 21 or older, the punishment is $25–$200 for the first offense and $100–$500 for subsequent offenses.

If you present a fake or altered driver's license or DPS identification card, you can be charged with a different statute, which is a Class C misdemeanor. In some cases, this may be filed as a felony. Lending your driver's license is also a Class C misdemeanor (for more information about this subject, see §§ 1.80–1.81).

2.65 *Public Intoxication.* A person, regardless of age, who is intoxicated to the degree that he or she is a danger to himself or herself or others and is in a public place, violates the law.

No sobriety tests are required. The officer's opinion is all that is necessary for an arrest. This offense is a Class C misdemeanor. In rare instances, the officer may choose to ticket you rather than arrest you.

2.66 *Open-Container Law.* It is illegal to drink and drive. This is a Class C misdemeanor.

2.67 *Prohibited Times for Public Drinking.* If you consume or possess with intent to consume an alcoholic beverage in a public place fifteen minutes after the bars close until 7:00 A.M., it is illegal. If it is on a Sunday, the prohibited time of consumption is extended until noon. This offense is punishable by a $50 fine. Most people get caught for this offense around 11:00 A.M. Sunday on Padre Island during Spring Break, but the law is enforceable throughout the state and throughout the year.

2.68 *Transporting Alcoholic Beverages into a Dry Area.* Know where the dry areas are in your town. If you are carrying more than 288 ounces of beer (one case) or more than one quart of liquor, you are presumed to be carrying it with intent to sell it illegally. This is a misdemeanor punishable by a fine of $100–$1,000 and/or one year in jail. The officer can arrest or ticket you and will usually take and keep the alcoholic beverages.

If you are not transporting it for sale but are charged with this offense, you must go to trial to convince a judge or jury that you had it for your own use. This will be difficult for you to do without an attorney.

2.69 *Alcoholic Beverages at Public Schools.* Possession of any alcoholic beverage on public school grounds, in public school buildings, or at public school athletic stadiums is a Class C misdemeanor.

This DOES NOT apply to state universities and colleges. Each university or college's governing board adopts rules controlling possession and sale of alcoholic beverages on its campus. The rules vary from campus to campus.

2.70 *Driving while Intoxicated (DWI).* It is illegal to drive a motor vehicle in a public place if intoxicated. *Intoxicated* means:

1. Not having the normal use of mental or physical faculties by reason of the consumption of *alcohol,* a *controlled substance,* a *drug,* or a combination of two or more such substances.

2. Having an alcohol concentration in your blood of .10 percent or more.

If stopped, you will be questioned and you *may* be given a road-side sobriety test (this is not required). If the officer decides you are intoxicated, you will be offered a breath test. You can ask for a blood test instead, but you can't demand it. If you refuse to take the breath test, your driver's license will be suspended for 90 days with no probation if you are 21 or older. If you are under 21, the suspension is for at least 1 year. If you go to trial, the fact that you refused can be told to the judge or jury. You do not have a right to talk to your attorney BEFORE taking the test. If you take the test and score .10 or higher, your license will be suspended for at least 60 days, regardless of whether you are prosecuted for DWI or not.

At the jail or police station, you will probably be video taped, especially if you refuse the breath test. This video can be shown at your trial.

The punishment for DWI is as follows:

1. Class B misdemeanor with confinement in jail for not less than 72 hours.

SPECIAL NOTE (probation): If it is your very first offense and no one was seriously injured or killed, there is a good chance you can have the jail time probated. Probation, successfully served, is NOT a conviction, unless you are convicted for DWI a second time.

2. If previously convicted of DWI *one time* (including probation), it is a Class A misdemeanor with confinement in jail for at least 30 days.

3. If previously convicted two or more times, it is a Third-Degree felony.

If there was serious bodily injury to someone else or a death or an open container of alcohol in the car, the fines and jail time increase.

You will also have your driver's license suspended for 90 to 365 days on the first conviction of DWI. This is a separate suspension from refusal to take the breath test, or scoring .10 or higher on the breath test.

Your insurance premiums will increase.

SPECIAL NOTE: Flying a plane or piloting a boat while intoxicated is treated the same as DWI.

2.71 *Intoxication Assault:* If you cause serious bodily injury to another while driving, flying, or boating while intoxicated, it is a Third-Degree felony.

2.72 *Intoxication Manslaughter:* If you cause the death of another while driving, flying, or boating while intoxicated, it is a Second-Degree felony.

Chapter 3
Living on Your Own

Living on your own presents an entirely new set of rights, respon-sibilities, and problems. Since you will most likely rent the first place you live, this chapter will set forth the rights, responsibilities, and problems of renting an apartment or house. Although I'll fre-quently refer to an "apartment," because that is the most common first rental residence, the same rules apply to a duplex or house.

3.1 *Oral Lease.* The oral or verbal lease is an agreement that is not written down. Most are simple agreements about the amount of rent and deposit. Oral agreements can have other clauses, such as how long you will live in the apartment, no pets, maintenance of yard, and so forth.

Oral leases have at least two major problems:

1. If no agreement is made on the length of time you will live in the apartment, the landlord only has to give you a 30-day notice to change anything. He or she can give you a 30-day no-tice and raise the rent, tell you to move for no reason, tell you to get rid of a roommate or a pet. You have one advantage in this type of agreement; to move out, you must only give a 30-day notice.

2. People can easily misunderstand the terms of the original agreement or fail to remember exactly what was said. This can create major problems and may end up costing you money.

EXAMPLE: You say you never agreed to live in the apartment for a specific period of time. After 4 months you give a 30-day notice that you will be moving out at the end of the fifth month. The landlord says you agreed to live in the apartment for 6 months and cannot move until the sixth month is up. With nothing in writing, it's a swearing match. If the landlord takes you to court for the rent for the sixth month, who will the judge or jury believe?

The bottom line is that the problems with oral leases outweigh any advantages. If the choice is up to you, it is better to insist on a written lease. If the landlord doesn't have a lease form, you can purchase one for a small sum from an office supply business that sells legal forms, or you could draw up your agreement yourself on ordinary paper in plain English. As long as it clearly states the agreement in ink and is dated and signed by you and the landlord, it will be considered to be a binding document.

3.2 *When Is It Okay to Have an Oral Lease?* When your written lease has expired and the landlord does not ask you to sign a new lease, it is probably okay not to insist on a written lease. You know the landlord; the landlord knows you. It is not likely under these conditions that the landlord will raise your rent each month or give you notice to move for no reason. However, he or she could if he or she wanted to.

SPECIAL NOTE: Sometimes certain terms of the lease carry forward, even though the lease has ended.

3.3 *Month-to-Month Tenancies.* This term means that you have not agreed to live in the apartment for any specific length of time. You pay rent monthly; you can give a 30-day notice to move or be given a 30-day notice to move, at any time. Usually, month-to-month tenancies are oral, but they can be written.

3.4 *The Law and Oral Leases.* If the oral agreement is month to month and doesn't cover certain things, the law steps in. For instance, the law says you must give one rent period notice if you wish to move, unless you have agreed otherwise. This means, if you pay rent by the month, you must give one month's notice (30 days). If there is no agreement to the contrary, you can give this notice on any day of the month. If you give notice on 11 May, then you can move out 11 June. You pay only 11 days of rent in June. This is called "prorated rent" and is calculated by dividing one month's rent by thirty to find the daily rate. Take the daily rate and multiply it by the number of days to give you the correct prorated amount.

With an oral lease, notices of move-out and needed repairs DO NOT have to be in writing, unless you have previously agreed that they will be. It is still a good idea to give these notices in writing, so there can be no confusion on when and whether they were given.

The landlord's lien (discussed in § 3.68) CANNOT be enforced if there was no written lease.

Certain other laws also apply, including laws concerning repair, eviction, deadbolt locks, deposit refund, ownership disclosure, and others. These will be discussed at length below, after the WRITTEN LEASE section, because the laws apply to both oral and written leases. Those sections that are starred (*) apply to both oral and written leases.

3.5 *Written Lease.* This document can be as simple as a handwritten paper setting forth the amount of rent for a fixed period of time, or as complicated as a lawyer-drawn four-page document in small print.

To be legal, the lease must be dated and signed by both the landlord and the tenant.

You are entitled to a copy of the lease. The typical lease includes names of all parties, the length of time that you will live in the apartment, how much rent is owed and on what day, whether pets are allowed, how to notify the landlord for repairs, the deposit amount, and how much notice is required before moving out.

The main rules to remember are:

1. READ THE LEASE BEFORE SIGNING IT. (I know it's long, boring, and the landlord is standing at your elbow, but READ it anyway.) This saves you from nasty surprises later on.

2. Be sure *all* blanks are filled in *properly.*

3. A printed lease CAN BE ALTERED, if *all* parties agree to it and initial and date the changes.

4. A printed lease can be *added to,* in writing, above the signatures, if initialed. A separate piece of paper for additions can be used if everyone signs and dates it.

SPECIAL NOTE: Almost all written leases have a clause that says NO ORAL AGREEMENTS are valid. This means that oral promise of a new carpet CANNOT be enforced unless you put it IN WRITING.

Below is a step-by-step guide to finding, renting, living in, and vacating an apartment.

Looking for an Apartment

An asterisk * before the section number and title means that the section applies to oral as well as written leases.

* **3.6 *Finding an Apartment*.**   You know to check the classified sections of your newspaper and the phone book's yellow pages under "apartments." You may not be aware of several other "helps."

1. ***Free apartment finders:*** Many cities have businesses whose function is helping you find the right apartment. They are usually listed in the phone book under "apartments." They can save you lots of telephoning and are *free*. If you rent an apartment through such an agency, your landlord pays them.

2. ***Apartment associations:*** Many cities have an association that prints a guide to members' apartments. This guide is free. You'll find the association in the phone book.

3. ***Tenant associations:*** Some major cities have tenant associations who may print a guide. Look in the phone book.

4. ***University or college guide:*** If you are a student at a university or college, check with your student government to see if they provide a guide.

* **3.7 *Discrimination*.**   It is *illegal* to refuse to rent to a person based on race, religion, country of national origin, or family status. If you believe you have been discriminated against in renting or in being evicted, contact the property owner first. If that does not resolve the situation, you can contact your local civil rights council and:

The Texas Commission on Human Rights
6330 Hwy. 290 East, Ste. 250
Austin, Texas 78723
    (512) 437-3450

You can also contact:

HUD—Fair Housing and Equal Opportunity (FHED)
P.O. Box 2905
Ft. Worth, Texas 76113-2905
    (817) 885-5521 or call toll free 1-800-669-9777

* **3.8 *Viewing your Apartment*.**   Ask to see the apartment that you might rent. The law requires that a vacating tenant allow his or her apartment to be shown. If the apartment is still occupied, it may be hard to imagine what you will be getting. Notice the floors, walls, countertops, appliances, and any furniture that will be yours. In most cases, WHAT YOU SEE IS WHAT YOU GET. If the landlord promises paint, new carpet, or curtains, GET IT IN WRITING so that you can enforce it. If the landlord WON'T put it in writing, the odds are that he or she is not certain that you will get a new carpet. If the new carpet is important to you, DON'T TAKE THE APARTMENT.

In older houses or apartments, notice evidence of prior problems, especially with plumbing. Evidence of water leaks under the sink or on the ceiling should cause you to closely question the landlord. Have repairs been made? Ask the current tenant, if you can. I repeat, WHAT YOU SEE IS WHAT YOU GET, especially in an older building.

* **3.9 *Beware of Model Apartments.*** Some apartments have a "model" apartment for you to view. No one has ever lived in this apartment, so it will be in perfect condition. Ask to see your actual apartment. If the landlord will not show it to you, you have to make a difficult choice. If the apartment complex is an older one, BEWARE. Your actual apartment may have many battle scars. If the complex is new, there is a better chance that your apartment will not disappoint you. The decision is yours.

3.10 *Applications to Rent.* Once you have seen the apartment and want to rent it, some landlords will require you to fill out an application to rent. This is the landlord's opportunity to check you out. The application will ask for financial information and references from previous landlords. Under most rental applications, once you sign the application, YOU HAVE AGREED TO RENT the apartment. The landlord is not bound to offer you the apartment, but you are required to accept it if he or she does offer it to you. DON'T FILL OUT AND SIGN THE APPLICATION unless you intend to rent the apartment.

* **3.11 *Deposit.*** Most landlords will require that you pay a deposit at the time you fill out the application. If there is no application, you will pay the deposit at the time you say you want to rent the apartment. This is called a "security deposit." When it is paid in advance, it is really a "holding" deposit. If there is no application, the deposit serves also as evidence of your agreement to rent the apartment. In return, the landlord agrees to hold the apartment for you and not rent it to someone else.

If you move in, this "holding" deposit becomes a security deposit to guarantee that you will abide by the lease and won't damage any property. More about that function later.

If you DON'T move in, YOU MAY LOSE ALL OR PART OF YOUR DEPOSIT. If the landlord finds a replacement tenant who moves in on or before the date your lease was to begin, the landlord must refund your deposit, but he or she can keep a cancellation fee if stated in the lease, or may withhold the actual expenses incurred in finding the new tenant.

If you find a replacement tenant acceptable to the landlord, you will get a refund of your full deposit. If no acceptable tenant is found, you will lose your ENTIRE DEPOSIT.

DON'T PAY A DEPOSIT UNLESS YOU ARE SURE THAT YOU WANT THE APARTMENT.

* **3.12 *Utilities.*** When pricing apartments to fit your budget, don't forget utilities. Some apartments are "all bills paid"; most are not. Ask the landlord what the average utility bill will be and add a $20 cushion. Most landlords tend to underestimate utility costs. If you want a really accurate amount, ask the tenant who is moving out. You should also check with utility companies to find out if you are required to post a deposit to receive service.

3.13 *All Residents Should Sign the Lease.* This is for your protection as much as the landlord's. Most leases have a "joint and several liability" clause. This is a legal phrase that means that each person who signs the lease is responsible to the landlord for the full amount of the rent, not just his or her one-half or one-third. It is better for the tenants to have *all* tenants legally bound to pay rent, not just one or two. If only one name is on the lease, that is the person the landlord will sue if the lease is broken. You don't want to be sued alone. Also, if a dispute arises between tenants, the one on the lease may be able to lock out any tenants who are not on the lease.

3.14 *Length of the Lease.* Don't sign a lease that goes until May 1998 if you plan to move out in December 1997. There can be serious consequences to breaking a lease by moving out early. They will be discussed in §§ 3.42–3.49. Shop around until you find the right length of time at the right kind of apartment. Be sure the correct length of time gets filled in on the lease so that there won't be any surprises later. DO NOT buy the landlord's story that he or she will let you out early, even though you must sign a lease for a longer period of time. The landlord may get run over by a truck tomorrow, and nobody else will know anything about your special move-out deal. Besides, most leases have that "no oral agreements" clause.

True Story Number Twelve

Susie Anyone is thinking of moving out of her apartment. She wants to be sure to get back her deposit. She goes to see the attorney for students at her college for advice. (This attorney's advice is free.)

The attorney says, "How long is your lease?"

Susie answers by holding her hands up about 14 inches apart. (She is showing the attorney the length of the paper the lease is written on!)

The attorney closes her eyes and stifles her laughter. "Earth to student. Earth to student," she says. "How long are you supposed to live in the apartment?"

"Oh," Susie says. "I don't know. The usual time, I guess."

"Susie, come back with the lease. I can't help you until I see what it says."

"Okay, if I can find it," says Susie.

The lawyer thinks to herself as Susie leaves, "Do you suppose she knows to look before crossing the street, or is she really from some other planet?"

---

* **3.15 Pets.** Be sure your lease says that pets are permitted if you've been told you can have one. Some leases have a "no pets" clause that must be crossed out and initialed. No landlord has to permit pets, so it's up to the landlord to regulate the size, weight, and type of pet permitted.

The landlord can also charge a pet fee or deposit. Be sure you understand whether the amount you pay is a refundable deposit or a nonrefundable fee or a combination.

If you pay a deposit, have a pet, and then get rid of the pet, don't be surprised if the landlord refuses to refund the deposit until you vacate the apartment. The landlord needs an empty apartment to assess damage and to see if it needs defleaing.

Living in an Apartment

* **3.16 Move-In Inventory 1.** Some apartments provide a form for this. Some don't. If there is no form provided, use a piece of paper. Room by room, note any existing damage, such as marks or holes in the wall, stains on floors, carpet, or countertops, torn shades or curtains, cracked windows, and chipped appliances. If it comes furnished, check out the furniture. Date and sign the list, then copy it. Give the landlord one copy to attach to your lease, and you keep the other.

A MOVE-IN INVENTORY KEEPS YOU FROM HAVING TO PAY FOR SOMEONE ELSE'S DAMAGE when you move out. It avoids fights over your deposit refund.

* **3.17** *Pay Your Rent on Time.* It saves you trouble and money in the long run. It also makes good points with the landlord that might come in handy later on. If you pay rent after the due date and grace period, if any, there is almost always a penalty. Read the lease to see what the late charges will be. Under most leases, failure or refusal to pay late fees can result in the late fees being deducted from your next month's rent. You will then have to pay the remaining amount of rent due or be evicted.

* **3.18** *Hot Checks.* Try to avoid this, but if it happens, be aware that you will have to pay a hot-check fee of up to $25. IN ADDITION, you will have to pay LATE CHARGES, because a hot check means the rent wasn't paid on time. Late charges run from the date rent was due until you pay it. As noted above, in most leases, if you refuse to pay the hot-check fee or late fee, it can be deducted from next month's rent. You will then have to pay the balance due on the rent or be evicted.

* **3.19** *Never Refuse to Pay Rent.* In Texas, it is illegal to refuse to pay rent under almost all circumstances. You can refuse to pay rent if you can't live in the apartment because of fire damage or tornado damage. YOU CANNOT REFUSE TO PAY RENT because A REPAIR HAS NOT BEEN MADE.

* **3.20**. *Deadbolt Locks.* You may require that the landlord install a new lock or change or rekey the old lock. Check your lease to see if this request must be in writing. Normally, the landlord has 7 days to honor your request. In some circumstances, a longer time may be okay. The landlord can require your roommates to approve the change. If a burglary, attempted burglary, or crime of personal violence has occurred at the apartment complex, the landlord must honor your request within 72 hours. The landlord can CHARGE THE COST TO YOU, unless the door or window has no lock on it at all or if it is a sliding glass door without a pin lock. You can be charged the costs of labor, EVEN IF the work is done by the landlord's maintenance man. If the landlord fails to fulfill your request, you may rekey or replace the lock and deduct the actual cost from the next month's rent. Attach a copy of the receipt to the next month's rent check. You may also seek a court order to make him or her do so and obtain a judgment against the landlord for any actual damages that you have incurred, plus one month's rent, plus $500, plus court costs and attorney's fees, AND you can terminate the lease.

* 3.21 *Smoke Alarms.* State law requires that all rented dwellings have a working smoke alarm. If it is battery operated, the battery must be working when you move in. During the time you live in the apartment, you must replace the battery if it wears out. If the alarm needs repair, the landlord must repair it, if you report it. If the landlord fails to install or repair a smoke alarm, you can get a court order ordering installation or repair plus any damages you have suffered, plus one month's rent, court costs, attorney's fees, plus $100. You can also terminate the lease.

* 3.22 *Noise.* When you live in an apartment or duplex, you are sharing very close living space with your neighbors. You have rights, but so do they. Loud noise at an unreasonable hour is a CRIME, as well as a *violation* of your lease. Act responsibly and avoid trouble.

If too much noise is being made, the manager or landlord should be contacted, if contacting the noisemakers directly has not worked. If that doesn't solve the problem, the police are the next step.

The law says making too much noise at an unreasonable hour is disorderly conduct. You are subject to arrest and a fine of up to $500. The party *host* is responsible for the noise level of his or her guests. The host is the one who will go to jail and may be evicted (see § 2.25 for further information).

* 3.23 *Damages.* Under most leases, written or oral, *you* are responsible to pay for any damage caused by you or *your guests.* If you refuse to pay, most *written* leases allow the landlord to apply rent paid by you to other amounts owed first. The landlord will apply the rent to the damages and then bill you for more rent. You must pay or be evicted.

Remember, the landlord DOES NOT have to allow you to make the repair. He or she can insist that it be made by a professional or the apartment maintenance person.

3.24 *Parking.* Most leases contain a statement that the landlord regulates all parking. Those regulations can change during the course of your lease if you are given notice. Be sure that you know what the regulations are so that you won't be towed.

* 3.25 *Owner's Name.* By law, the manager must give you the owner's name and address and the management company's name and address if you request it. Read your lease. Some leases require that you make this request in writing. The manager has seven days to provide this information. In the alternative, the manager can

choose to keep the information posted in or near the office or provide the information with your lease.

If the manager *fails* to provide the information after the seven
days, you can get a court order requiring the landlord to disclose the
information. You can also get a judgment against the landlord for
damages, one month's rent, plus $100, court costs, and attorney's
fees. You can also terminate the lease.

* **3.26** *Utility Interruptions.* Utilities can be interrupted in two
ways, and the solution to the problem is different in each case.

1. *When you pay utilities:* The landlord CANNOT interrupt the
utilities except for repairs, construction, or an emergency. If the
landlord violates this, you may terminate the lease and recover
from the landlord actual damages, one month's rent *or* $500,
whichever is greater, and reasonable attorney's fees and court
costs, less any delinquent rents.

2. *When the landlord pays utilities:* If you get a notice from the
utility company that the utility will be cut off for nonpayment
by the landlord, you can:

a) Pay the utility company and deduct from your rent the
amount paid. Be sure to provide a receipt for this to the
landlord.

b) Terminate the lease with written notice within 30 days
of when you get notice from the utility of a future cutoff or
actual cutoff; you may deduct your security deposit from
the rent and recover a pro rata refund or any advance rent.

c) Sue in court for actual damages including moving costs,
reconnection fees, storage fees, and lost wages, along with
court costs and attorney's fees.

* **3.27** *Property Insurance.* GET SOME! As a general rule, the
landlord is NOT responsible if you are burglarized, have a fire, have
water pipes burst, or have a severe roof leak. The landlord *is* responsible if the problem occurs because of the landlord's negligence. The
landlord is negligent if the fire starts in his or her boiler room where
newspapers were stored, but not if your next-door neighbor has a
grease fire. The landlord is negligent if you have reported the lack
of locks on your windows and that's how the burglar got in. If the
burglar kicked in the locked front door, the landlord is not negligent. The first time the pipes burst or the roof leaks, the landlord is

not negligent. If it is the second or third time for the leaks, and faulty repairs have been made in between leaks, then the landlord may be negligent.

The bottom line is that most losses are your problem, not the landlord's. Property insurance is cheaper than you think and can be a real lifesaver. Check the yellow pages of the phone book under insurance and start calling. This insurance is usually sold in $1,000 increments, which is $5,000 worth of coverage, $6,000 worth, and so forth. You may have to talk to several companies before you find one that is willing to sell you a policy for the amount of coverage you want. Remember, insurance pays VALUE OF THE ITEM DESTROYED, NOT REPLACEMENT COST. If you want replacement cost, it is usually available for an extra fee.

SPECIAL NOTE: DO NOT ASSUME that your PARENTS' homeowner's policy automatically covers you if you live away from home. Check it out. Many homeowner policies cover you if you're a student living in a *dorm* but not if you live off campus.

* **3.28 *Furnishing Your Apartment.*** Milk crates, cinder blocks, and wooden boards are a great way to create bookcases or other storage. *However,* don't be tempted to take lumber, bricks, or cinder blocks from construction sites without permission. This is THEFT. The seriousness of the theft depends on how much you steal. An amount under $50 is a Class C misdemeanor, punishable by a $500 fine. From $50 to less than $500 is a Class B misdemeanor, punishable by a fine of up to $2,000 and/or up to 6 months in jail. From $500 to $1,500 is a Class A misdemeanor, punishable by a fine of up to $4,000 and/or up to one year in jail.

You would be surprised how few cinder blocks and 2 × 4's it takes to equal $50. You would be arrested if caught.

A special statute deals with milk crates bearing dairy company logos. Theft of milk crates is a Class C misdemeanor, punishable by a $500 fine. If you are in possession of a milk crate marked with a dairy's name, you are assumed to have stolen it. Attempting to scratch out or remove the dairy's name is also an offense.

Saving a few bucks is not worth the risk. Buy your own milk crates.

* **3.29 *Landlord's Right to Enter.*** He or she can enter at all reasonable times for any legitimate purpose. He or she is NOT required to give you advance notice that he or she will enter, UNLESS it is so stated in your lease. You can NEVER change the locks and refuse to give the landlord a key. You are only the renter. The landlord is ei-

ther the owner or represents the owner and *must* be allowed entry. You CANNOT insist that the landlord enter only when you are there.

Repairs

It is illegal to refuse to pay rent because the landlord has not made repairs. In most cases, it is also illegal to make repairs on your own and deduct the charges from your rent. Below are some steps that are legal.

* **3.30** *Giving Notice on Needed Repairs.* Always give notice of needed repairs *in writing*, note the date, and keep a copy. This prevents later arguments over whether notice was given and when it was given. This first notice determines all further steps that you can take to get repairs made. Besides, most leases require that the notice be in writing.

Most landlords will repair if all they receive is oral notice, in spite of what the lease says. The one time you rely on the oral notice and give no written notice is bound to be the time the repair does not get made. If your lease requires written notice, the landlord has a *legal excuse* for not having made the repair. So, bottom line: GIVE WRITTEN DATED NOTICE.

SPECIAL NOTE: Call in emergencies, but follow with a written notice.

True Story Number Thirteen

Susie has decided to stay in her apartment, if she can get the heater "fixed." She notifies the manager in writing that the heater does not adequately heat the back bedroom. The maintenance man comes but can find nothing wrong with the heater. Susie and the manager go round and round, arguing about the heater. The manager says the heater is working properly. Susie says that she is still cold.

Finally, Susie goes to see the attorney for students again. This time she remembers to bring her lease. (Of course, this time it isn't needed.) She explains the problem.

"Let me get this straight," says the attorney. "The heater is working, but your bedroom is too cold."

"Right," says Susie. "You see, the heater and air conditioner are combined in a single unit, mounted in the living room window."

"You mean, the hot air just blows out of that unit. There are no heating ducts to the bedroom?" asks the lawyer.

"Right," says Susie.

"So, you want the landlord to add heating ducts for the bedroom?"

"Right! It's too cold," says Susie.

"Susie, that is not a repair. That is asking for an alteration to the apartment. Even if the bedroom is too cold for you, the landlord has no duty to change the heating system. You rented the apartment with that type of heater, so you are stuck with it," says the lawyer. "The landlord is *not* required to alter it. There has been no breach of the lease."

---

* **3.31 *How Much Time Does the Landlord Have to Make a Repair?*** He or she has "reasonable" time. What is "reasonable?" It depends on the problem. If the dishwasher won't work, three or four weeks is reasonable. If you have no water, no hot water, or no working toilet, one or two days is reasonable. It really depends on the seriousness of the problem and the availability of parts and labor. If the heater is broken, but it is May, the landlord has more time to fix it than he or she would have in January. If you think reasonable time has lapsed, call the landlord to find out what the holdup is.

* **3.32 *If Reasonable Time Has Lapsed and the Repair Has Not Been Made.***

1. Go over the head of the local manager to his or her supervisor, the management company, or the apartment owner. Remember, you have a RIGHT to the owner's and management company's names and addresses (see § 3.25).

2. Complain to the local apartment association if your landlord is a member.

3. Complain to the local tenant's association if there is one.

4. If you are a student at a college or university that provides a legal counselor for students, enlist that person's help.

5. Complain in writing to the local BBB and to the nearest Texas Attorney General's Office for Consumer Affairs (see §§ 7.1 and 7.2 for details).

6. If the above remedies fail, there is a law that sets forth a procedure to follow. You send a SECOND notice of repair, giving the landlord seven days to make the repair. If he or she fails to do so, you can cancel the lease and move out, getting back your deposit and prorated rent, IF the needed repair is MATERIAL TO YOUR HEALTH OR SAFETY. What does "material to your health or safety" mean? In this case, "material" means IMPORTANT, so the phrase means "important to your health or safety." This could include broken door locks, broken toilets, no heat in the winter, no air conditioning in the summer, and so forth. This means you can't cancel the lease because the dishwasher is broken or the faucet is dripping and repairs haven't been made.

7. If you don't want to move out, the statute allows you to sue the landlord for a court order that orders the landlord to:

a) Make the repair.

b) Reduce your rent until the repair is made.

c) Pay your actual damages, court costs, and attorney's fees.

d) Pay you a penalty of one month's rent plus $500.

SPECIAL NOTE: Suing your landlord is an extreme remedy. You may win your case, but you may make the landlord very angry with you. Future relations may be unpleasant. Be sure that you are willing to live with this unpleasantness before you sue.

8. When you can make the repair and deduct it from your rent:

a) If the landlord so agrees.

b) If the landlord has failed to remedy the backup of raw sewage inside the apartment or the flooding from broken pipes or natural drainage, and you've given notice of your intent to repair.

c) If the landlord has agreed to furnish water but you have none, and three days have lapsed since notice that you would make the repair.

d) If the landlord has agreed to furnish heating or cooling and it is not working properly, *and* the landlord has been notified in writing by the appropriate local authority (housing, building, or health) that the lack of heat or cooling *materially* affects your health or safety, and three days have lapsed since giving notice of your intent to repair.

e) If an appropriate official has notified the landlord that the condition materially affects the health or safety of an ordinary tenant, and seven days have passed since you gave the landlord notice of your intent to repair.

Such repairs must be made by a professional, not by you or your relatives (unless the landlord agrees). You cannot have repairs made that cost more than the amount of rent you owe. You must provide receipts to the landlord. To invoke any of these remedies, you must *owe no back rent.*

* **3.33** *Legal Delay of Repair.* The landlord can give a sworn statement (affidavit) to the tenant to legally delay his or her duty to repair:

1. For 15 days if the delay is caused by obtaining necessary parts for which the landlord is not at fault.

2. For 30 days if the delay is caused by a general shortage of labor or materials following a natural disaster, such as tornado or hurricane.

* **3.34** *Landlord Can Sue You.* If you refuse to pay rent because repairs have not been made or you deduct the cost of repairs improperly from your rent, the landlord can sue you for actual damages and one month's rent plus $500.

Roommates

The landlord-tenant laws say nothing about roommates. Leases usually do. As stated earlier, all people who sign the lease are responsible to see that *all* of the rent gets paid to the landlord, not just that person's one-half or one-third. The agreement to share rent, space, and other bills is between the roommates only. It does *not* involve the landlord. The landlord usually retains the right to insist on a single check for rent payment, and he or she may issue only one deposit refund check after you move out. Notice of intent to move out is usually treated as notice from *all* roommates, even if it is only signed by one. The landlord can treat you as one family.

Other problems that may arise between roommates are as follows.

* **3.35** *Nonpayment of Bills.* All too often, one deadbeat roommate takes advantage of responsible roommates by not paying his or her share of the bills. If it is rent, the unpaid balance must be paid, or all roommates will be evicted. If it is the phone bill or electric bill, the bill must be paid to continue service. The utility expects payment from the person whose name is on the bill.

To avoid or minimize these problems, try the following. Don't get all of the bills in one roommate's name. You get the electric bill in your name, and let your roommate get the phone bill in his or her name. Then you have a hold on each other. If a deposit must be posted to get utility service, *all roommates* should contribute equally. If a guarantor is going to guarantee payment of the phone bill, instead of posting a deposit, get the phone in your name, BUT get your roommate's parents to guarantee the bill. That way both families are involved.

If you do get stuck with your roommate's part of the bill, you can sue your roommate in small claims court. Unfortunately, that is not a very good solution (see § 7.4 on small claims court for further information).

* **3.36 *Lending Money.*** DON'T. Avoid this problem by refusing to lend money, especially if it is a large amount. Deadbeat roommates will never pay you back. Since it is difficult to tell the deadbeats from the good guys, play it safe. Don't lend an amount that you can't afford to lose.

* **3.37 *Sharing Space.*** If you've never lived with this person before, it's a good idea to lay down some ground rules. Be smart and put them in writing. Areas to cover in your agreement are:

1. Paying bills.

2. Who uses what bedrooms, bathrooms, and shelves in the refrigerator.

3. Whether you're willing to share food, stereo, TV, VCR, or clothes.

4. Can boy/girl friends sleep over or not, and if so, for how many days running.

You can probably think of other areas, too. An agreement from the beginning can save arguments later.

* **3.38 *Moving Out Early.*** If your roommate disappears and the rent is due, you will have to pay the entire amount or move. The landlord might be willing to give you some extra time to pay the rent or find a new roommate if you've been a good tenant.

If you have to move, you will lose your deposit. The landlord can sue either of you or both of you. (More information about the consequences of breaking a lease is given in §§ 3.42–3.49).

If you stay and pay the extra rent, you can sue your ex-roommate for it, but collecting the money may be difficult (see §§ 7.4 and 7.5 on small claims court).

* **3.39 *Buying Things Together.*** I mean sofas, VCR's, TV's, and so forth. It is probably better not to, but if you do, write an agreement at the beginning. The agreement should say how you are going to pay for the item and how you are going to divide the item when you split up. A written agreement can save headaches later.

* **3.40 *Getting Rid of a Deadbeat Roommate.*** Legally, *you* cannot evict a roommate *whose name is on the lease,* deny him or her entry to the apartment, or hold property of that roommate hostage to collect a bill, unless the roommate agrees.

If you want the roommate out, you must work it out between you or talk to your landlord.

If the roommate's name is NOT on the lease, talk to the landlord. The landlord may be willing to lock your roommate out, BUT you must permit the roommate to take his or her stuff.

* **3.41 *Deposits and Multiple Roommates.*** If roommate A moves out and roommate B remains and gets new roommate C, what happens to the deposits? There is NO LAW on this, so it is up to the landlord. Check the lease first. If it says nothing, then usually the landlord either forfeits A's deposit for breaking the lease or tells A that A can get his or her deposit back when everyone moves out. Usually the landlord will require C to post a new deposit.

Sometimes the landlord tells A to get the deposit money directly from C, and the landlord will refund A's old deposit to C at the end of the lease.

It is really up to the landlord. You have no control over this. Be sure everyone understands what is going to happen.

Moving Out Early

If you have decided that you must move before your lease expires, be aware of the consequences. Although these sections are starred, they only apply to an oral lease if you fail to give a 30-day notice of move-out or if your lease was for a specific period of time.

* **3.42 *Reasons for Breaking a Lease.*** Except for failure to make certain repairs (see §§ 3.30–3.34), there is seldom a *legal reason* to break the lease. A roommate moving out, illness, loss of job, or quitting school DOES NOT give you a *legal* reason to move.

* **3.43** *Deposit or Cost of Reletting.* Read your lease. Most leases have a clause that forfeits the deposit if you break the lease and move out early.

Some leases have a cost-of-reletting charge. The amount of the cost-of-reletting charge may be more than your deposit. It will be charged if you break the lease. Your deposit will be deducted from it, and you will owe the remaining balance. Charges for cleaning and damage can be deducted from the deposit first. The remaining deposit is then deducted from the cost of the reletting fee, and you will owe the balance.

* **3.44** *Rent Owed.* Breaking the lease also makes you liable for the rest of the rent due under the lease. If your lease ends 31 May, but you move out on 31 March, you owe the rent for April and May.

The landlord should make a reasonable attempt to rerent the apartment. If he or she has a new tenant move in the first of May, then your lease is cancelled at that point. You owe rent only for April.

If the apartment remains vacant, in spite of the landlord's attempt to rerent it, you owe rent for the remainder of your lease—in this example, April and May.

Will your apartment get rerented right away? Consider these circumstances. Are there other empty apartments in your complex? The landlord does not have to rent your apartment first. If the complex is full, there's a better chance that your apartment will get rented quickly. Also consider what time of year it is. More people move at the end of May, end of August, and end of December. If you can time your move out at one of those times, you increase the chances that your apartment will be rented quickly.

Give the landlord as much notice as you can that you will be moving out. This lets him or her know that your apartment will be available to rent. He or she may get it rerented before you move out; then you won't owe any rent.

* **3.45** *Collection of Money Owed the Landlord.* To collect rent and cost of reletting owed him or her for your early move out, the landlord can do any of the following:

1. Bill you repeatedly himself or herself.

2. Turn your name over to a collection agency and let the agency attempt to collect from you.

3. File the debt on your credit report, thereby giving you bad credit for seven years.

4. Report you as a lease-breaker to a business that keeps track of such tenants. This might make renting more difficult in the future if your new landlord checks your references with them. (Note: Not all cities have this type of business.)

5. Sue you in court.

* 3.46 What Is the Landlord Likely to Do? The greater the amount of money owed to the landlord, the more likely the landlord will pursue you for the money. So, if the landlord gets the apartment rerented quickly and you owe him or her only $200, it is less likely that he or she will use all of the steps listed above.

* 3.47 What If the Landlord Sues? Many landlords do not sue because it costs them some money for filing fees and an attorney. The other reason the landlord may not sue is the difficulty of getting blood from a turnip. You're the turnip and the "blood" is money. In other words, the landlord may sue and win a judgment of not only the rent owed but his or her attorney's fees and court costs, BUT the landlord may never be able to collect anything from you because you don't *own* anything.

Texas law allows a single person $30,000 worth of personal property ($60,000 if you are married) that cannot be seized to pay a judgment debt. Personal property is everything but land. For most young people, $30,000 covers everything they own.

SPECIAL NOTE: The $30,000 covers your car, furniture, clothing, and so forth, BUT it does NOT cover savings accounts, certificates of deposit, or *large* checking accounts. If your checking account just barely covers your monthly expenses, it is *probably* protected.

Because of this difficulty in collecting a judgment, many landlords choose not to sue. *However,* some landlords WILL SUE anyway, hoping that someday you will have property.

* 3.48 Are Your Parents Responsible? Not if you were 18 or older when you signed the lease AND your parents DID NOT *cosign* or guarantee the lease.

* 3.49 Roommates. If one roommate moves out, the remaining roommate must pay the additional rent or find a new roommate. Failure to do so means the remaining roommate must move out, too. The landlord can pursue both of you for breaking lease, EVEN THOUGH it is really the first roommate's fault. Legally you are both responsible. This is not fair, but it is the law.

SPECIAL NOTE: For those of you thinking that it might be better to get *evicted*, read §§ 3.67–3.70 on eviction. The bottom line is that you *still owe the rent*, even if you are evicted.

Proper Move-Out Notice

Your lease expires in one month or it has already expired, and you are living on a month-to-month basis, or you're on an oral lease that is month to month and you want to move out legally. What do you do? Follow the steps below.

* **3.50 *Give Your Move-Out Notice.***   In most cases this will be a 30-day notice. If your lease says a different amount of time, follow the lease. If you're on an oral lease, you must give one rent-paying period's notice. Usually you pay rent monthly, so it will be a 30-day notice, but if you pay rent every two weeks, then give two weeks' notice.

Give the notice in WRITING. This is *required* by most written leases. It is not required in an oral lease situation, but it is still the best way to go.

Date the notice and keep a copy.

Under many written leases you MUST give notice on the *first of the month*. If so, be sure it is on the *first*. Even if you don't pay your rent until the third, give your notice on the *first*. If you give it on the third, a picky landlord can say that he or she DID NOT get *30* full days' notice and refuse to refund your deposit.

If your lease does not specify notice on the first or if you are not on a written lease, you can give your notice on any day. You can give it on 13 April to move out on 13 May. The landlord must then allow you to pay rent for only the first 13 days of May.

SPECIAL NOTE: Remember, a notice to move out from *one* roommate is taken by the landlord as notice *from all roommates*. The landlord assumes *everyone* is moving out and will rerent the apartment. If only one roommate is moving out and the remainder are staying or getting a new roommate, check with the landlord. Probably no notice of move-out is necessary because the apartment won't be vacated.

However, if one roommate gives notice and the landlord assumes that *all* of you are moving out and then rerents the apartment, he or she can INSIST that you *all* move.

* **3.51 *Ask for Cleaning Instructions.***   Some landlords include them with the lease. Others hand them to you when you give your

move-out notice. Still others have none. Generally speaking, cleaning means just that, including scrubbing handprints off walls, vacuuming out window sills, cleaning appliances, especially the oven, and shampooing the carpet. Some landlords also want all nail holes filled in.

3.52 *Special Cleaning Fees in the Lease.* Some landlords reserve a certain amount of your deposit for a "cleaning fee." Find out from the landlord what this fee is for. Sometimes, it is for carpet cleaning. If it is, you don't need to clean the carpet too. Sometimes it is just for "cleaning." It will be deducted, even if the apartment is spotless. It is legal to do so because you agreed to it when you signed the lease.

* 3.53 *Get the Landlord to Walk through with You.* This way the landlord can point out anything that is not acceptable. You'll have another chance to clean it.

If the landlord can't or won't walk through with you, get a non-roommate friend to notice whether it is clean. If a dispute arises over cleaning, this friend can be a valuable witness in court. If you're a guy, let the friend who walks through be a female. A prejudice still exists, well-founded or not, that females know more about cleaning than males.

* 3.54 *Damages Versus Normal Wear and Tear.* The landlord *cannot* charge you for "normal wear and tear," but he or she *can* charge for damages. Sometimes it is hard to tell which is which.

If the carpet was new when you moved in three years ago and you have kept it clean with no stains, but it has begun to pack down in the traffic areas, that is normal wear and tear. You shouldn't be charged for it. If, on the other hand, you spilled red fingernail polish on it, that is damage, and you can be charged.

In case a dispute arises as to how serious the damage was, TAKE PICTURES for future use in court. Photographs can settle many arguments.

* 3.55 *Move-In Inventory 2.* Remember this? I told you about it back in § 3.16 when I talked about moving in. Now it becomes valuable. Ideally, before the landlord charges you for any damage, he or she should check his or her copy of the move-in inventory and be sure the damage was not done by a previous tenant. If the landlord fails to do this and charges you for something already noted on the move-in inventory, then produce *your copy* of the move-in inventory and point out the damage. This should resolve that charge.

* **3.56** *Return All Keys Promptly.* The landlord might be able to argue that you haven't really moved out until all keys are returned. You might end up owing several days of rent for however long you've kept the keys.

Some written leases have a specific charge for late key return.

* **3.57** *Give the Landlord Your Forwarding Address.* Until all roommates have done this, the 30-day period for refund of the deposit DOES NOT start. All such addresses should be given IN WRITING.

* **3.58** *Single Deposit Refund for Multiple Roommates.* Check your lease. Some landlords reserve the right to make only *one* refund check and send it to one roommate. Sometimes they put *all roommates'* names on the check. Sometimes they put only *one*. Find out the landlord's policy. You want *all* roommates' names on the check, so that all of you must sign the check to cash it.

If you have a dishonest roommate who gets the check and signs your name to cash it, you can file *felony forgery* charges against him or her. Your complaint is against the roommate, NOT the landlord.

* **3.59** *Deposit Refund.* Once you have given proper move-out notice, cleaned, moved out, turned in keys and given your forwarding address, the landlord has 30 days to refund your deposit. He or she must put in writing the deductions and the reasons for the deductions. Deductions can be made for inadequate cleaning and damage. Deductions cannot be made for normal wear and tear.

* **3.60** *Disputes over Cleaning or Damages.* When you get the itemized list of deductions, attempt to discuss any problems with the landlord. If this does not resolve the situation, you may then choose several courses of action against the landlord. You can file a complaint with the BBB; the Texas Attorney General's Office for Consumer Affairs; the local apartment association, if your landlord is a member; a tenant association, if there is one in your town; the dispute resolution center, if your area has one; or file suit in small claims court. (Information about the dispute resolution center and small claims court is in §§ 7.3–7.5.)

Once in court, the burden is on the landlord to prove that his or her charges are reasonable. If you win, you are entitled to your court costs and attorney's fees.

In a dispute, your eyewitness who checked the apartment for you and any photographs you took can be of great value (§ 3.54).

* 3.61 *No Refund or Itemized List after 30 Days.* First call the landlord to find out what the problem is. If this doesn't solve the problem, you can file suit against the landlord in small claims court. Under the SPECIAL PENALTY STATUTE, the landlord is presumed to be acting in *bad faith* if the refund or itemized list hasn't reached you within 30 days. *You may then sue the landlord for three times the deposit plus $100.* If you win, you are entitled to your *court costs and attorney's fees* as well.

At trial, the landlord must show the court why he or she was late and that he or she was not acting in bad faith. If the judge or jury finds that the landlord *did* act in bad faith, no deductions can be made from the deposit for any cleaning or damage. You will be awarded three times the full amount of the deposit plus $100 plus attorney fees and court costs.

If the landlord convinces the judge or jury that he or she had a good reason for being late with the itemized list or refund, then deductions can be made for lack of cleaning and damages, if the landlord proves such charges reasonable. Obviously, you get to dispute the charges. In this case, the most the court could award would be the full deposit, court costs, and attorney fees. The landlord could countersue for additional amounts if claimed damages are more than the deposit.

The longer it has been past the 30 days, the harder it is for the landlord to show a good reason for being late.

True Story Number Fourteen

Susie Anyone finally moves out of her apartment when the lease is up. She gives proper move-out notice and her forwarding address to the manager. She waits for her deposit refund.

Six months pass with no refund and no written explanation. Susie calls the manager many times. Each time the manager assures Susie that she will get her full deposit back in just a couple of weeks.

Finally, Susie goes to the attorney for students. The attorney talks to the manager, but no money appears. The attorney advises Susie to file suit in small claims court (see § 7.4) on her own without a lawyer. The filing fee is $65. Susie sues for three times her $150 deposit ($450) plus $100 for a total of $550, as allowed by statute, since the deposit is now five months past due.

The hearing date is set. Susie discovered that her old manager has hired a lawyer. In a panic, Susie returns to the attorney for students. The attorney reassures Susie that she can handle this case without a lawyer.

"I guarantee, Susie," says the lawyer, "that you will know as much or more than her lawyer does about this statute. Here is a copy of it. Most lawyers seldom deal with this kind of case, because there is little money in it. All you have to prove is proper move-out procedure, that you gave your forwarding address, that it is past thirty days since you moved out, and you've received neither your deposit refund nor a written statement. You then explain why you sued for $550, and your job is finished. The manager must then explain to the court why she has waited so long to refund your money. If she doesn't have a good reason, the money is yours. It is very hard to come up with a good reason to withhold both the money and a written explanation for five months. If by some strange chance, the manager does convince the judge that she had a good reason, then you won't get the treble damages and extra $100. You still have a good chance of getting your basic deposit," says the attorney.

"You really think I can do it on my own?" asks Susie.

"Yes, Susie, even you can do this. Come back after the hearing and let me know how it turns out," says the attorney.

"Okay," says Susie.

After the hearing, a jubilant Susie returns to the attorney for students.

"I won it all," she shouts. "It was just like you said. I proved my part. Her lawyer tried but couldn't get her to give a good reason for withholding my deposit. The judge awarded me all $550. When her lawyer asked the judge why he was awarding treble damages, it was obvious the lawyer didn't know about the statute. I volunteered to show her lawyer my copy of the statute. It was great. And I got my court costs, too."

If Susie Anyone can win a case like this, so can you.

SPECIAL NOTE: Remember, you have to have followed proper move-out procedure to use this statute.

* 3.62 *Withholding Your Deposit from the Last Month's Rent.* DON'T! A special statute says that if you do, the landlord can *sue* you for *three times* the wrongfully withheld rent, winning also court costs and attorney's fees.

* **3.63** *Foreclosure.* If the mortgage holder has repossessed the apartment complex from your landlord, it is your *old landlord* who owes you a deposit refund, not the mortgage holder. You can sue your old landlord for the deposit, but the odds are that you'll never collect anything because he or she has no money.

SPECIAL NOTE: A forecloser can demand a new deposit from you, demand that you move out giving you a 30-day notice, or demand that you sign a new lease.

* **3.64** *Bankruptcy.* If your landlord has filed for bankruptcy, you become a creditor of the landlord, just like everyone else. It is your landlord who owes you the deposit. You should receive a Proof of Claim form from the bankruptcy court or trustee to file with the court. If you don't get such a form in the mail, contact the nearest federal bankruptcy court for the form. You can fill it out yourself. The filing is free and can be done by mail. The odds are not good that you will ever see your money.

* **3.65** *Sale of Property.* If your apartment complex has been sold to a new owner by your old owner, voluntarily (not through bankruptcy or foreclosure), normally your old owner will transfer your deposit to the new owner, and it is the new owner who will refund your deposit. You are supposed to be so notified by your old landlord, but he or she may forget.

There are some cases where deposits are not transferred to the new owner, and you must go back to the old owner for your money. You find this out from the new owner.

If the new and old owners are batting you back and forth like a Ping-Pong ball and none of the help agencies can resolve it, sue both landlords in one suit, and let the court resolve it.

Generally speaking, a new owner must honor any lease still in effect when the owner buys the property.

Eviction and Other Steps to Force You to Live Up to Your Lease or to Move Out

The most common reason for being evicted is nonpayment of rent. Most of the actions described in this section deal with that. However, you can be evicted for any "material" breach of the lease. This includes having noise complaints against you, violating the no-pets rule, having people not on the lease living in the apartment without the landlord's consent, and many other things. I'll indicate which paragraphs apply to eviction for reasons other than failure to pay rent.

* **3.66 *Notice on Your Door.*** This is a polite, or not so polite, note left by your landlord to remind you that you owe rent. Many landlords leave such a note as a first step. There is no requirement that this type of note be given.

* **3.67 *Lockout.*** Some landlords skip the polite note and go straight to a lockout. To lock you out, the landlord must first give you a warning letter—at least 3 days before locking you out—telling you the date that you will be locked out if you fail to pay your rent. If by the date stated in the letter you still have not paid, the landlord must leave a note on the door, telling you where you can get a key, 24 hours a day. When you go to get the key, the landlord can ask you why you haven't paid your rent. Regardless of *whether you pay rent or not,* the landlord MUST GIVE YOU THE KEY to get in. A lockout serves as a way to confront you, NOT as a way to EVICT you. If you don't pay the rent due after you've been locked out once, you can be locked out again. In fact, you can be locked out each time you leave until you pay the rent. The landlord must always give you the key to get back in.

Landlords use this to confront you and annoy you so much that you'll pay the rent.

If the landlord fails to let you into the apartment, you can:

1. Get a court order that allows you back in the apartment.

2. Recover from the landlord actual damages, one month's rent or $500, whichever is greater, attorney's fees and court costs, *minus* the late rent owed by you.

SPECIAL NOTE: Any clause in the lease that says you give up this right is invalid.

3.68 *The Landlord's Lien: Taking Your Possessions Hostage.* To use this, there must be a WRITTEN LEASE and that lease must contain a paragraph called the LANDLORD'S LIEN. The paragraph must be underlined *or* printed in boldface type (bigger and darker than the rest of the lease). It must say that all nonexempt property can be seized and held until you pay the rent due.

If you are behind in rent and the landlord's lien is in your lease, the landlord can come into your apartment and take nonexempt property (usually TV's, VCR's, stereos, and so forth). You must be left a note listing the items taken, the amount of rent owed, and where it should be paid. The notice must also say that the items will be returned when the rent is paid.

The landlord may take property with a value greater than the amount owed.

If some of the property taken belongs to someone else who does not owe rent, the landlord must release that property to its rightful owner after being shown *proof of ownership.*

If you fail to pay the rent, the landlord may SELL the property. He or she must give you 30 days' notice of the sale by both first-class mail and certified mail, return receipt requested, to your last known address. The notice must give the date, time, and place of sale, an itemized list of the amount you owe, and the name, address, and phone number of the person to contact regarding the sale. It must also state your right to get the property back if you pay. You can pay right up to the moment of sale.

After the sale to the highest bidder, proceeds of the sale must be applied to the amounts you owe. If there is money left over, it must be sent to your last known address by certified mail not later than 30 days after the sale.

If the landlord violates this procedure, you can sue for actual damages, return of any property that has not been sold, return of the proceeds of any sale, and one month's rent or $500, whichever is greater, minus any amount of rent you owe, plus attorney's fees.

Exempt property or property that *cannot* be seized includes:

1. Wearing apparel.

2. Tools, apparatus, and books of a trade or profession.

3. School books.

4. Family library.

5. Family portraits and pictures.

6. One couch, two living-room chairs, and a dining table and chairs.

7. Beds and bedding.

8. Kitchen furniture and utensils.

9. Food and foodstuffs.

10. Medicine and medical supplies.

11. One automobile and one truck.

12. Agricultural implements.

13. Children's toys not commonly used by adults.

14. Goods the landlord knows are owned by someone not a tenant.

15. Goods the landlord knows you are still making payments on with a finance company.

Remember, the landlord's lien must be in WRITING and underlined or in bold print to be in effect.

SPECIAL NOTE: A statement in your lease that says your landlord CAN seize any of the above items is VOID. This statute cannot be changed by your lease.

If the landlord has tried all of the above and you are still behind in rent, *or* if the landlord wants to skip all of the above, he or she must give you an eviction notice.

* **3.69** *Eviction Notice.* This must be in writing and give you three days to vacate. A written lease may alter this time period. This notice must be delivered by mail, either first class or certified or delivered in person, to any person on the premises who is 16 years old or older, or it may be left attached to the inside of the main-entry door. The three days begin on the day notice is delivered. If you fail to move out, the landlord must file a suit for eviction.

* **3.70** *Suit for Eviction.* The steps necessary to evict you through a court proceeding are outlined below. This lawsuit is called by the old common-law name of "forcible entry and detainer" or just "forcible detainer." It *means* a suit for eviction.

1. The landlord files the suit with the justice of the peace court asking for your eviction and any past-due rent.

2. You are served a copy of the papers by the sheriff's deputy or constable. The papers can be left with anyone 16 years or older at your home. If unable to find you, the papers can be mailed to you or attached to your door.

3. You can move out at this time voluntarily and not go to the hearing. If you fail to appear at the hearing and the landlord sues for back rent, the landlord will win a judgment against you, awarding him or her the rent. Of course, he or she may win the judgment for back rent, even if you do appear.

4. The hearing date noted in the papers served will be no sooner than 6 days and no more than 10 days from the date notice of suit is served. The hearing will be in front of the judge alone, unless you request a jury trial. To have a jury trial, you must request one, paying the jury fee of $5.00 within 5 days of when you are served.

5. At the hearing, the landlord will tell his or her story first, explaining how you violated the lease. You tell your story next. The judge or jury decides if you are in violation of the lease and if you owe any back rent. If it is decided that you broke the lease, the judge will issue a judgment against you.

6. The judgment gives you 5 days to leave the apartment with all of your property (except for items held by the landlord under the landlord's lien for back rent).

7. At the end of 5 days, if you have not left, the judge will issue a WRIT OF POSSESSION. This WRIT empowers the sheriff's deputy or constable to REMOVE YOU from the apartment, physically if necessary. If you won't remove your property, the landlord will, under the deputy's or constable's supervision.

The items removed can be set outside but not on a public sidewalk or street and not in rain, sleet, or snow. The landlord CANNOT BE REQUIRED TO STORE your property. The deputy or constable can hire a warehouseman to remove and store your property AT YOUR EXPENSE.

SPECIAL NOTE: If the landlord *does* store your property removed under a writ of possession, he or she can hold it HOSTAGE until you pay back rent and storage fees, if so stated in your lease. All of the property can be held HOSTAGE, because it was NOT seized under the special landlord's lien.

8. Judgment in the justice of the peace court can be *appealed* to the county court for a NEW TRIAL by filing an appeal bond with the justice court within *5 days* of the hearing. You will need an attorney for this.

* **3.71 *Eviction for Public Indecency Conviction.*** If you use the apartment for prostitution, promotion of prostitution, display of obscenity, sale or distribution of obscene material to a minor, sexual performance by a minor, or if you possess or promote child pornography, and you are convicted of one of those offenses and all of your appeals of the conviction are abandoned or exhausted, you can be EVICTED. The landlord must give you 10 days' notice to move, regardless of your lease.

* **3.72 *Abandonment of the Apartment.*** The landlord is entitled to assume you have abandoned the apartment if most of your possessions are gone and you do not sleep in the apartment for a reasonable time. Some leases say the apartment will be presumed abandoned if you are gone more than five days without informing the landlord of your whereabouts, if you have removed most of your property.

   Abandonment lets the landlord go in and gather up any remaining possessions, store them, and get the apartment ready to rerent, *even if your rent is paid up to the end of the month.* If you intend to return to get the remaining items and clean up, TELL THE LANDLORD. Otherwise, you may have to pay for any cleaning the landlord has done.

   The landlord can hold abandoned items HOSTAGE for back rent and *maybe* for storage fees. Check your lease.

Chapter 4
Personal Relationships

4.1 *Common-Law Marriage.* A common-law marriage is a marriage that has had no official wedding ceremony. Children born are legitimate. Property acquired during the marriage is community property under most circumstances. To end a common-law marriage, you must file for divorce.

How do you create a common-law marriage? By living together for a reasonable period of time, *holding yourself out to others as being married.*

What is a "reasonable" period of time?

There is no magic answer. Probably two weeks is enough; probably two days is not enough. The time in between is in limbo. In other words, it is up to the courts. The judge or jury could find two or three days as a reasonable time or not, depending on the individual circumstances.

What is "holding yourself out to others as being married"?

This means that the woman uses the man's last name. You introduce each other as wife and husband. You have a checking account for Mr. and Mrs.; you sign your lease Mr. and Mrs.; and you seek credit as Mr. and Mrs. In other words, you act like you are married.

What if you tell only your landlord that you are married, because you know that he or she will not rent to you otherwise, but to your friends you say you are just living together?

Probably you don't have a common-law marriage, but the more places you put your names as Mr. and Mrs., the more likely you are to create a common-law marriage.

What if you have filed for dependent status with the U.S. Armed Forces or have filed a joint tax return with the IRS?

You have a common-law marriage.

SPECIAL NOTE: If the common-law marriage comes to an end, you should file for divorce within one year.

4.2 *Just Living Together.* If you live together openly and never tell people that you are married, then no common-law marriage exists, regardless of how long you live together. Children are not automatically legitimate but can be legitimated through the courts. Property purchased together is jointly owned. There is no legal process necessary to end this relationship. This makes it easy to walk away, BUT if there are children or you cannot agree on a property division, the end can be messy. If the parents of children split without agreeing about support, it may be necessary to go to court for a support order or to prove paternity. A court action can be used to divide any jointly purchased property. Anything bought solely with your own salary is your separate property to keep.

Because of all the potential problems, lawyers don't recommend living together as a long-term relationship, especially if children are born (see § 4.1 above to determine if you have a common-law marriage).

4.3 *Paternity.* If you father a child, you have responsibilities to that child that can be enforced in court, if necessary, even if you never marry the mother.

1. *Before the child is born:* As the father, you have no legal rights before the child is born. You have no right to demand an abortion or prevent one. You have no control over whether the mother smokes, drinks, or has adequate medical care. You also have no legal duty to provide money for medical expenses. However, after the child is born, if you are named the father by the court, you can be ordered to pay one-half of the birth medical expenses along with child support.

2. *After the child is born:*

a) *If the mother keeps the child:*

(1) If you admit that you are the father, you are agreeing to take on the responsibility of child support until that child is 18. It is a good idea to do this through a court paternity proceeding so that the amounts are spelled out and you have visitation rights.

(2) If you do not admit that the child is yours, the child's mother can file a PATERNITY suit against you to try to prove that you are the father. This is done through

testimony (yours, hers, and any other witnesses) and blood tests. Blood tests can be ordered by the court, if necessary. You should hire an attorney to represent you if sued for paternity. If found to be the father, you can be ordered to pay support until the child is 18 and be granted visitation rights. You can be sued for paternity any time until the child reaches age 20.

(3) The mother can ask you to give up all rights and responsibilities to the child by signing a "Waiver of Interest." You give up your rights FOREVER and have no duty to pay support.

b) *If the mother puts the child up for adoption:*

(1) If you don't want the child yourself, you will be asked to sign a form called a "Waiver of Interest" or an "Affidavit of Relinquishment" giving up your rights FOREVER. You'll have no contact with the child and no duty to support the child.

(2) If you do want the child, you must hire a lawyer and intervene in the adoption proceeding. If you admit to being the father and the mother admits it, you have a better chance to get the child than strangers would. However, if the child's mother would rather keep the child herself than let you have it, she will probably get to do so.

4.4 *Child-Support Amounts.* As the parent of a child, you must provide support for that child until the child is 18, or longer if the child is disabled.

The noncustodial parent will be ordered by the court to pay a specific amount of support, usually monthly, whether the child is legitimate or not. The minimum amounts of support are set by law as follows:

1. One child: 20 percent of net income.

2. Two children: 25 percent of net income.

3. Three children: 30 percent of net income.

4. Four children: 35 percent of net income.

5. Five children: 40 percent of net income.

6. Six or more: not less than the amount for five children.

Net income means gross pay minus income tax withholding, social security (F.I.C.A.), and insurance coverage for the child, if so ordered. You can *agree* with the other parent on a different amount of child support.

4.5 *Child Visitation.* The parents may reach their own agreement, but if they do not, a statute sets the visitation for the noncustodial parent.

The statute provides specific times if the parents live less than 100 miles apart or more than 100 miles apart. Since the statute goes into great detail, it is beyond the scope of this book. If you wish to read the statute, go to the reference section of the public library and ask for the Texas statutes. Look in the second volume of the Family Code at §§ 153.312 and 153.313.

4.6 *Community Property.* Texas is a community property state. Any salary you earn is community property if you are married at the time you earn it. It belongs one-half to you and one-half to your spouse. Anything you purchase with that salary becomes community property. Any other income you receive while you are married, such as interest on a savings account, is also community property, even if the savings account itself is your separate property (see § 4.7 for definition of separate property). In fact, there are only two common ways to obtain separate property while you are married. The ways are as a gift or as an inheritance.

You can agree to keep income as separate property, if you sign a prenuptial agreement before you marry. You need an attorney for this.

Upon divorce, community property is divided by the spouses, or if no agreement can be reached, by the judge or jury. Generally speaking, each party is entitled to one-half of the assets.

Debts are also treated as community if incurred while married, unless only a spouse's separate property was used as collateral. This is a lengthy subject with many possible variations. If you are involved in a divorce with disputes over property or debts, HIRE A LAWYER.

4.7 *Separate Property.* Any property you own before marriage remains separate property after marriage, as long as you can trace it. If you confuse it with community by mingling the two together, you may not be able to claim it as separate property later in a divorce. Inheritances and gifts made solely to you are also separate property, even if made after marriage.

Separate property need not be considered in making an equal division of community property.

4.8 Wedding Gifts.   Generally speaking, wedding gifts given to both the bride and groom are treated as community property. They belong one-half to each spouse, regardless of whose relative gave the gift. The court will divide them equally if you don't reach your own agreement.

If a wedding gift, such as lingerie, was given to one particular spouse, then it is that spouse's separate property.

4.9 Gifts between Boyfriend and Girlfriend.   If you are dating someone and give that person various gifts, you do NOT have a *legal* right to demand a return of those gifts when you break up.

4.10 Engagement Rings.   In almost all cases, if the wedding is called off, the ring must be given back to the giver. This is because an engagement ring is a *conditional* gift, not an absolute gift. It is conditional on the marriage taking place. If the giver doesn't want the ring back, it doesn't have to be returned.

4.11 Legal Separation.   There is no such thing in Texas. You are either married or divorced. You must separate to file for divorce and live apart during the time the divorce is pending, but this "separation" is not a legal status.

Some states have three separate categories—married, legal separation by court decree, and divorce. Texas doesn't.

4.12 Divorce.   This is a complicated and lengthy subject, beyond the scope of this book, but I will give you some basic information.

> **1. *Grounds (reasons) for divorce:*** Texas has a no-fault divorce system that only requires that *one* party wants out. This party must be willing to swear to incompatibility under oath in court. The old grounds of adultery, cruelty, abandonment, and so forth are still on the books but seldom used. There is no reason to use these "fault" grounds. Generally, the court's job in a divorce is NOT TO PUNISH THE OTHER PARTY but to end the marriage. If you insist on filing the divorce under one of the "fault" grounds, you will find your attorney's fees are extremely expensive.

> **2. *One attorney cannot represent both parties:*** An attorney can represent *only one* spouse, even if the other spouse is not contesting the divorce and doesn't hire an attorney.

3. *Must you hire an attorney to get a divorce?* No, if you have no kids and no property. Several "how-to" books are available at bookstores. The books are inexpensive and provide the forms needed with instructions. If you have kids or property, *you must hire an attorney.*

4. *Alimony (spousal support):* There is temporary support during the time the divorce is pending and permanent support for up to 3 years, if the marriage lasted at least 10 years and the spouse is not able to be self-supporting. You must hire a lawyer to get alimony, and it is granted only in certain instances.

5. *How long does it take?* The divorce petition must be on file for 60 days before a final hearing can be held. It may take longer than that for various reasons.

4.13 Annulment. This is dissolution of a marriage as though it never existed. The process is very similar to divorce and costs the same or more. Annulment is *only* allowed in the following special circumstances:

1. Underage, or less than 18 years old when married without parent's permission IF filed within 90 days of the marriage, as long as the minor has not turned 18.

2. Marriage under the influence of alcohol or drugs.

3. Impotency.

4. Marriage through fraud, duress, or force.

5. Mental incompetency.

6. Concealed divorce.

7. Marrying a relative that is too close.

True Story Number Fifteen

"What can I do for you?" the lawyer asks.

"I want a divorce or annulment or out somehow. It was all a terrible mistake. Wanda Sue and I ran off and got married, even though our parents didn't want us to. Now, I can see that they were right," says Joe Anyone.

"How long have you been married?" the lawyer asks.

"One week," Joe replies.

"*One week!* Don't you think you're being a little hasty? Lots of people need a little while to adjust to each other."

"No, I know it isn't going to work. I want out as painlessly and cheaply as possible," says Joe.

"Are you both eighteen?" asks the lawyer.

"Yes."

"Then you will probably have to have a divorce, not an annulment. It is a lot easier and cheaper to get into marriage than it is to get out of it. I can file the papers quite soon, but the law requires that the final hearing can't be held until the sixty-first day after filing," says the lawyer.

"Whatever you say. My mind is made up. I want out," says Joe. "What will it cost?"

Once more, acting hastily has gotten Joe in trouble. Once more, he is making his lawyer richer.

Chapter 5
Consumer Credit

The state of your credit can be of prime importance to you in our society. It can affect not only your ability to obtain a loan or a new credit card but also your ability to rent an apartment or get a job.

This chapter contains information about your credit history, the collection of debts, and what rights you have if you are being contacted by a debt collector.

5.1 *Credit-Reporting Agency.* This is a private company that records your credit both good and bad. The agency is supported by merchants who pay to be members and who pay to get credit reports. Besides listing bad things like court judgments, past-due accounts, and late payments, good credit is listed as well.

Bad things stay on your credit history for seven years. Bankruptcy stays on your credit history for 10 years.

Some lenders or credit card companies will give you new credit, even if you have some bad credit, but most will not.

You can view a copy of your credit history by paying a small fee. If you have been denied credit because of something bad on your credit history, you can ask to see your credit history for free, if you do so within 30 days of the denial.

5.2 *Before Your Debt Goes to a Collection Agency.* It is much easier to make a deal with the creditor you owe money to than a collection agency. Explain in writing what you can afford to pay monthly, and enclose the first payment to show good faith. Include a description of how much money you make each month and what your other debts are. The creditor is far more likely to accept your monthly payments if he or she can see that there is no way you can pay more. Don't put in writing anything that you don't intend to do. Don't skip payments. Even if the creditor refuses this arrangement over the phone, try it in writing. You have nothing to lose, and sometimes the creditor will accept.

Do not expect a creditor to give you any special consideration because you quit your full-time job to go to school. That was your decision, and when you made it, you knew that you owed money.

Do all of this before a collection agency is involved. Once one is involved, you must deal only with the collection agency. The creditor will not intervene.

Collection agencies are much less likely to accept a monthly installment agreement for small amounts of money. They will want all of the amount owed at once or in large installments. Sometimes they will offer to settle for less than the full amount of debt owed if paid all at once.

5.3 *Collection Agency.* Do not confuse a collection agency with a credit-reporting agency. A collection agency is a private company which may be hired by a creditor to collect money from you. Sometimes a single company may be *both* a collection agency and a credit-reporting agency.

Collection agencies will contact you by phone and by mail, repeatedly if necessary, to try to get you to pay what you owe. There are laws regulating what kind of contact is allowed. They will be discussed in following sections.

Once the debt is at the collection agency, you must deal with the agency. It is usually too late to make a deal with the merchant. Most collection agencies want the full amount now. If they agree to installments, it is almost always three or four large ones. Sometimes they may be willing to settle for less than the full amount if you can pay the entire settlement at once. Be sure to get such an agreement in writing.

Do not let a collector keep you on the phone wasting both your time and his or hers. If you can't pay, say so and politely hang up. For further information on what collectors can and can't do, see the following sections.

If unable to collect from you, the next step is suit in court (see § 5.11 for further information).

SPECIAL NOTE: The following rules apply to the collection agency, not necessarily to the creditor. The creditor may or may not have to follow the same rules. If in doubt about the actions of a creditor, contact the Texas Attorney General's Office for Consumer Affairs (see § 7.2 for addresses).

5.4 ***Written Notice from the Collection Agency.*** By law, the notice from the collection agency (hereafter called "notice") must state the amount of the debt, the name of the creditor, and a statement that you have 30 days to dispute the validity of the debt or the debt will be assumed to be valid.

If you wish to dispute the debt, you must do so in writing, within 30 days. The collection agency must then obtain verification of the debt or judgment. The agent must send this verification to you along with the name and address of the original creditor. Until this information is mailed to you, the collection agency cannot attempt to collect.

The notice cannot appear to be a document issued by a court or governmental entity. It cannot appear to be from a law firm or an attorney, unless it really is.

5.5 ***Threats, Harassment, or Abuse.*** A collection agency cannot:

1. Threaten violence.

2. Threaten to accuse or accuse someone falsely of fraud or another crime.

3. Tell or threaten to tell a third party that a debt is undisputed if you have disputed the debt in writing.

4. Threaten arrest or the filing of criminal charges for nonpayment where no crime has been committed.
(SPECIAL NOTE: This doesn't prevent the filing of hot-check charges if a hot check was issued.)

5. Publish a list of debtors who have refused to pay.

6. Advertise the sale of a debt in an attempt to force payment.

7. Threaten to take property without a proper court proceeding UNLESS such property is COLLATERAL (see § 5.15).

8. Use profane or obscene language.

9. Phone without disclosing the collection agency's name with willful intent to harass or annoy.

10. Cause the phone to ring repeatedly or make repeated phone calls with intent to harass.

11. Communicate by postcard.

12. Cause you to pay for collect telephone calls without having disclosed the debt collector's name.

5.6 *When Calls Can Be Made.* By federal law, calls must be made only between the hours of 8:00 A.M. and 9:00 P.M. in your time zone.

5.7 *Calling You at Work.* You can be called at work. If you want to stop this, the next time they call, have your supervisor tell the collection agency that you cannot receive such calls at work. The collection agency must stop or violate the law.

5.8 *Postdated Checks.* It is illegal under federal law to:

1. Threaten to deposit a postdated check early.

2. Ask for a postdated check with intent to threaten criminal prosecution.

3. Ask for a check postdated more than 5 days *and* fail to give written notice of intent to deposit the check not more than 10 nor less than 3 business days prior to such deposit.

As stated in § 6.4, postdated checks can cause many problems. I do not recommend giving one to anyone, ever.

5.9 *Getting the Collection Agency to Leave You Alone.* If you notify the collection agency *in writing* that you refuse to pay the debt and that you want the collection agency to end all further contact with you, then all contact must stop. Send this notice certified mail, return receipt requested (see § 6.16), so that you can prove it was received. Keep a copy of the letter.

Once you do this, the agency can contact you *only* to tell you that they will stop all contact or to tell you that a lawsuit will be filed. This is a federal law.

5.10 *Penalties for Breaking the Law.* If the collection agency breaks a Texas law, there are two possible penalties.

1. *Criminal:* A conviction of a misdemeanor with a fine of $100–$500. This is very seldom used, but does exist.

2. *Civil:* A private civil lawsuit can be filed by you and your private attorney.

3. *Best Course:* Before you try to see the district attorney to file criminal charges or hire an attorney, contact the TEXAS ATTOR-

NEY GENERAL'S OFFICE FOR CONSUMER AFFAIRS (see § 7.2 for addresses). Their services are free. They can file a suit on behalf of the entire state if enough complaints are received.

If a federal law has been broken, you can also file a civil suit through your own attorney. You can recover your actual damages, punitive damages up to $1,000, and attorneys' fees. If you are part of a class action suit, the penalties are greater.

Even if you think only a federal law has been violated, file a complaint with the Texas Attorney General's Office. They can help.

True Story Number Sixteen

Sam Anyone has gotten himself into debt. He had a good job and was able to get several credit cards with high credit limits. Human nature being what it is, he charged to the max. Then Sam lost his job. He has a new job, but it doesn't pay very well, and he was out of work several months. He fell behind in his payments. Now he has a collection agency after him, trying to collect the money. Sam has no way to pay anything but small installments. He goes to see the attorney for students.

Sam tells the attorney his sad story. The attorney tells Sam the information you have just read in this chapter.

Sam says, "Well, what about the collection agency calling me at home and keeping me on the phone for one hour? It made me late for work. Can I stop that?"

"Why did you let the person keep you on the phone?" asks the lawyer.

"Well, I didn't want to be rude. I had a hard time interrupting. He kept asking me questions and wouldn't believe my answers."

"Sam, once you have explained your situation to the person, say, 'There is no point in talking any further.' Say goodbye. Then hang up. I know your mother taught you to be polite on the phone, but use some common sense. That man is trained to keep bugging you until you pay. It's silly to let him keep you talking. Interrupt. Say goodbye and HANG UP. There is such a thing as being too polite."

5.11 *After a Collection Agency.* If unable to collect the money from you, the next step is suing you in a court of law. Generally, this will be in a court in your hometown, unless there is a previous agreement to the contrary, such as a credit cardholder's agreement. You will be served papers by a sheriff's deputy, private process server, or by certified mail.

You have the right to represent yourself, but you may be better off with an attorney to represent you. You will have to hire the attorney yourself. In some cases the local legal aid office may be able to help you (see § 7.10 for more information).

If it is a debt you owe, you are going to lose with or without an attorney. An attorney can help you if the debt is in dispute. If it is not, an attorney can help you minimize the amount of attorney's fees the creditor can get. Of course, you may not save much in the long run, if you have to pay your own attorney.

5.12 *Collecting a Court Judgment.* You cannot go to jail for failure to pay a court judgment. Under Texas law, a debtor has certain protections.

If you own or are buying your home, it CANNOT be taken away to pay a judgment, unless the judgment is for taxes, the mortgage on the home, or for a home-improvement loan on the home. This is the homestead law.

Texas law also allows you to have $30,000 worth of personal property ($60,000 if you are married) that cannot be taken away from you to pay a debt. Personal property is anything but land.

Texas has an additional law that protects your car, furniture, family pictures, children's toys, household pets, and tools of your trade from being seized. These items are added together to reach the $30,000 exemption. These items are NOT protected from seizure if they were used as collateral on a loan (see § 5.15 about collateral).

Wages cannot be garnished. The Texas Supreme Court has held that once you deposit your wages in a checking account, they are no longer "wages" and can be taken. The Court seems to indicate that you will be left enough money to pay bills but that any excess can be garnished to pay a judgment debt.

Savings accounts, certificates of deposit, and stocks and bonds are NOT protected and can be taken.

5.13 *Must the Creditor Attempt to Collect the Judgment?* No. Some creditors put the judgment against your credit, file a lien against any land you own (hoping you own something besides a homestead, which is protected), and wait. The creditor hopes to receive payment when you are trying to straighten out your credit.

5.14 *Interest on a Judgment.* The law currently allows a minimum of 10 percent per year on a judgment. This is usually less than the prejudgment interest you were charged on an overdue credit card account.

5.15 *Secured Creditor and Repossession.* If you borrow money to buy a car, a piece of furniture, a stereo, or a like item, you almost always sign an agreement to pay the money with the item purchased listed as collateral. This is called a "security agreement." The collateral is the "security" that the loan will be repaid. All security agreements have a paragraph in which you agree that the named item (car, stereo, and so forth) can be taken from you if you fail to pay. This is called "repossession." The statute discussed in § 5.12 about protected property DOES NOT apply in the case of repossession. If you have a security agreement, Texas allows the creditor to take the named item without a court order. You have the right to refuse to let the creditor in the house to repossess your stereo.

If you do so, the creditor must get a court order to allow entry to seize the stereo. You can be made to pay the creditor's cost of obtaining that court order if so stated in the terms of your loan agreement.

You must be given a reasonable period of time to pay the entire amount of the note (not just catch up on payments due). If you do not pay to redeem the item, it will be sold. The sale proceeds must be applied to the amount you owe and costs of the sale.

SPECIAL NOTE 1: Sale proceeds of used merchandise almost *never* cover the entire amount due on the note. *You still owe the remaining balance.*

SPECIAL NOTE 2: A secured note does not have to be for the purchase of an item. If you need to borrow money for some other reason, it is common to have you list items on the note for collateral. These nonpurchase money agreements are treated exactly the same as purchase money agreements.

SPECIAL NOTE 3: BEWARE of making late payments. Just because the creditor allowed a late payment last time DOES NOT mean he or she will allow it this time. Under most agreements, the creditor reserves the right to repossess ANYTIME you are late or delinquent, EVEN though he or she didn't do it the first time.

Chapter 6
Employment and Consumer Concerns and Other Issues

This chapter contains brief legal information on a variety of topics.

Employment

6.1 *Getting Fired.*   Under Texas law, you can be fired for no reason. There is no requirement that you be warned first or that you have done anything wrong. Also, severance pay is *not* required.

This rule has some exceptions.

1. *Contract:* If you are employed under a union contract or another written agreement, your contract probably sets forth the way you can be fired. Read it and find out. If it doesn't, then you can be fired as stated above.

2. *Company policy:* All government agencies (municipal, county, state, or federal) and some private businesses have written procedures for firing. Generally, you can only be fired for doing something wrong, and frequently you must be warned first. Businesses are not required to have such a procedure, but if the business has imposed on itself a procedure, then it must be followed. Usually, this procedure is set forth in an employee handbook or policy statement. If you don't have a handbook, ask your personnel office for one. If there is no handbook, there is usually no procedure.

SPECIAL NOTE: You cannot legally be fired for refusing to break the law if your boss orders you to do something illegal. However, he or she can wait and fire you later for no cause.

6.2 Discrimination. It is illegal to fire, refuse to promote, or refuse to hire based on race, religion, sex, or color. Problems of discrimination in employment can be reported to your local human or civil rights commission. If there isn't one or you are not satisfied with the results, report to:

Texas Commission on Human Rights
6330 Hwy. 290 East, Ste. 250
Austin, Texas   78723
   (512) 437-3450

This complaint needs to be in writing. You can also complain to the federal Equal Employment Opportunity Commission at the following addresses:

8303 Elmbrook   4171 N. Main St.
Dallas, TX   75247   El Paso, TX   79902
   1-800-669-3362   (915) 534-6550

1919 Smith Street, 7th Fl.   5410 Fredericksburg Rd.
Houston, TX   77002   Suite 200
   1-800-669-4000   San Antonio, TX   78229
                                     1-800-669-4000

Complaints to these agencies are free. You may also have grounds for a private civil lawsuit. You must find your own attorney for this. Most attorneys will take this kind of case on a contingent-fee basis—that is, they receive their pay from your winnings, if any. You have to pay filing costs, win or lose. Remember, lawsuits can win big bucks but can take a long time.

SPECIAL NOTE: Discrimination on the basis of age or handicap is permitted in some situations if done on reasonable grounds. Complaints in these two areas should be made to the same agencies noted above.

6.3 Sexual Harassment. It is illegal to sexually harass an employee. What constitutes sexual harassment? Certainly, requiring sexual favors for promotion or to retain a job is clearly sexual harassment. Other things include inappropriate language, touching, and an atmosphere that intimidates a worker. The only way to stop such harassment is to COMPLAIN to the highest-ranking supervisor possible. If the employer fails to correct the situation, you can complain to the Equal Employment Opportunity Commission at the addresses given in § 6.2 above. Such complaints can also be made to the Texas agencies noted in § 6.2. If all else fails, or if you are not satisfied with the results, you may hire your own lawyer and file a civil lawsuit. A lawyer may be willing to represent you on a contingent-fee basis—that is, no fee from you unless you win your lawsuit (for more information on contingent fees, see § 7.8 [3]).

Consumer Concerns and Other Issues

6.4 *Postdated Checks.* Don't give one. It is not illegal to do so, but it is unwise. Banks hate them. Problems occur when the check is deposited too early. Either it bounces because your account is empty, or it causes other checks to bounce because you weren't expecting it to be deposited. You are stuck with charges either way.

Technically, the bank is supposed to look at the date and refuse to cash it until the due date. As a practical matter, the bank seldom notices the date and frequently accepts the check. Legally, the bank is responsible if it cashes the check too soon or bounces it too soon. The bank should drop any bank hot-check charges. The bank should also give you a letter to show anyone else who has charged you, saying that it was a banking error. If the bank paid the post-dated check, the bank should restore the money to your account. On the date the check is due, the bank CAN REMOVE THE MONEY FROM YOUR ACCOUNT. It is very difficult to get banks to do this.

This is a problem that is easy to avoid. Just don't give any post-dated checks.

6.5 *Three-Day Right to Cancel a Written Contract.* You have the right to cancel *certain* contracts even though you signed them.

Home-solicitation contracts for *$25 or more* can be canceled. Notify the other party in the manner noted on the contract that you wish to cancel. You have three business days after signing. Always do so in writing and send it certified mail, return receipt requested (see § 6.16) so that you can prove it was received. Keep a copy of your letter. Be sure it will be postmarked by midnight of the third business day.

Home-solicitation contracts clearly include door-to-door sales. Whether such contracts include telephone sales is not clear. It is safest to assume they do not, so don't rely on the three-day right to cancel for phone sales. Also, the three-day right to cancel does not include a door-to-door salesman who gives you a coupon that you must go into his business place to use. The sale is then taking place in a store, not your home.

Health-spa contracts also must have the three-day right-to-cancel clause, even though they are not a "home solicitation." More about health-spa contracts in § 6.6.

6.6 *Health-Spa Contracts.* State law regulates health-spa contracts by requiring certain clauses in the contract and forbidding certain practices.

As of 1985, there can be no "lifetime contracts." A special contract price must be available to all comers, not a select few, but it can be for a limited time or for a specified number of people, like the "next 50 callers."

The contract *must* contain the following clauses or paragraphs set forth in bold print.

1. *Three-day right to cancel:* As noted in § 6.5 above, the contract must contain this right with instructions on how to do it. Be sure to send the notice certified mail, return receipt requested, and be sure to send it on time.

2. *Health-spa closing:* If the health spa CLOSES, it must send you a statement telling you where to send notice of your cancellation. This cancellation right doesn't exist if the spa provides you with another similar facility that will accept your membership with no transfer fee and that is within 10 miles of the old spa.

3. *Your poor health, injury, or death:* In case of disability or death, the contract can be canceled. The spa may require proof of disability or death. A prorated refund will be made if the fees have already been paid in full.

If the contract does not contain these three clauses in bold print, you can cancel the contract. The spa may be subject to other penalties as well.

6.7 *Refunds on Merchandise.* There is *no* law that requires a business to give you a refund if you decide you don't want the item, whether it is five minutes after you buy it or two weeks later. No refund need be made.

Many large businesses will refund your money if you decide you don't like the color, but many will not. It is very common for smaller businesses to offer an exchange or credit in the store rather

than a refund. They do not have to do even that. There is no requirement that a sign be posted stating this policy or that the receipt
have the policy printed on it.

If a new item is defective, you MUST be offered a refund. If it
is a used item, there is no requirement to refund. You buy used
items, as is.

Electronics stores, ski equipment stores, and the like seldom
give refunds. Before you make the purchase, be sure you really want
and can afford the item.

True Story Number Seventeen

Joe has some really terrific stereo equipment, but he'd like to
upgrade it. A local stereo store advertises the very component he
wants at a special sale price. It will take all of his spare cash, but
it's worth it.

Joe goes to the store, talks to the salesman, and examines the
advertised component. Joe gets into a technical discussion with
the salesman. He tells the salesman what results he expects, using
the new component. The salesman says that Joe will be disappointed with that particular component because it won't do what
Joe wants. What Joe *really* needs is a different component that
costs more and is not on sale (naturally).

Joe is very disappointed. He really wanted to upgrade his
equipment. He'd already told all of his friends how it was going to
sound. Now he'll have to confess he was wrong about the advertised component.

The salesman offers Joe a really good deal on the more expensive component. Joe hesitates. It still costs more than the advertised component, but it is a good deal, and his stereo will sound
great. In short, he talks himself into it.

As he is carrying the boxed component to his car, he has second thoughts. What will he eat for the next month? He's spent all
of his food money plus his spare cash on this component. Common
sense reasserts itself, and Joe realizes that he has made a mistake.
He turns around and returns to the store with the unopened box in
his arms. It has been almost one minute since he paid for the
component.

Joe asks for his money back, explaining his problem. To his
horror, the cashier points to the sign on the cash register. "No
refunds." It also says that on his receipt. They will exchange the
merchandise for something else, but he can't have his money
back.

Unfortunately, Joe will have to get his nourishment from great-sounding music for the next month. The store does not have to give a refund, since the merchandise was not defective.

6.8 *Layaways.* Many stores offer this service. Be sure you understand the terms of this agreement. Know how often you must make a payment and how long the layaway lasts.

If you miss a payment, the item can be returned to the shelf and sold to someone else for the full price. You are not entitled to a refund of any sort.

Pick up layaways promptly once the final payment is made. Stores are not in the free-storage business.

6.9 *Late Billings.* If the bill comes late, do you still have to pay? YES! If the phone company bills you for the first time *one year* after you made the long distance calls, YOU STILL OWE THE MONEY. If the first bill is more than four years late, then you can claim that the bill is past the statute of limitations. Remember, that only means they can't win if they take you to court. It can still go against your credit.

6.10 *Credit Card Responsibility.* It is very unwise to lend your credit card to anyone, even your best friend. If you give your friend permission to use the credit card to buy gas, and he or she uses it for other things as well, you *may* be responsible for those additional purchases if your friend does not pay you.

If your credit card is lost or stolen, you are responsible for only $50 of the purchases made by the thief. You must notify the credit card company of the loss or theft as soon as possible. This also applies to automatic teller cards.

It is wise to be very careful about using your credit card for telephone purchases, *if the merchant calls you.* While many such companies are reputable, some are not. Sometimes products are not as represented. Sometimes the amount billed to your credit card is more than the amount you authorized. *If you call the merchant,* it is unlikely you will experience such problems.

If you do have a problem with a merchant on a credit card purchase, first attempt to correct the problem with the merchant. If you are not satisfied, you may contact your credit card company for assistance if:

1. The purchase is for more than $50.

2. The purchase is made in your home state or within 100 miles of your mailing address.

Even if you don't meet those conditions, try your credit card company. They may be willing to help.

Remember, you must notify the credit card company about *billing errors, in writing,* within 60 days of receiving the bill.

It is a FELONY to use a credit card without permission (see § 2.44 for further information).

6.11 *Power of Attorney.* This is a piece of paper signed before a notary public in which you give someone the power to act for you. The legal term for the person who is going to act for you is "attorney." This does not mean, of course, that the person must be a licensed attorney. It can be anyone 18 years old or older.

A general power of attorney means that the person you have named as your "attorney," can sign your name and in general do anything on your behalf. This person could sell your car, write checks on your account, and so forth. Obviously, you only name someone you trust.

A special power of attorney is a document that empowers your "attorney" to do only a specific act, like sell your car.

Forms for this can be obtained from any large office supply company that has legal forms.

A power of attorney can be for a specific stated period of time or for an indefinite time—that is, until you revoke it.

Powers of attorney do not need to be registered anywhere to be valid, but you can register a power of attorney with the county clerk. If you do register it, then you must revoke it in writing and register the revocation. If you don't register it, you can revoke it by tearing it up.

The person (attorney) who is going to use the power of attorney on your behalf must have the original, notarized document. A copy will not do.

6.12 *Car Repair.* See §§ 1.105–1.124.

6.13 *Lemon Law.* See § 1.92.

6.14 *Buying a Used Car.* See § 1.93.

6.15 *Video Tapes.* If you rent video tapes, you are responsible for their return. If you fail to return the tapes or return them late, you are responsible for the daily rental rate for each day late until the cost of the tape is reached. Then you must pay the cost of the tape. The same is true for VCR rental. You may be subject to additional charges if you signed an agreement when you rented the tape or VCR. You may be sued in court to recover this money. You may also be subject to criminal charges (see § 2.40).

6.16 *Certified Mail Return Receipt Requested.* Use this type of mail to prove that the mailed item is received. Address your envelope in the ordinary manner, but do not put a stamp on it. Go to any post office window and ask for this service. It costs less than $2.00. You will be asked to fill out a postcard with your name and address on it. This postcard will be returned to you with the receiver's signature. It proves the letter was received.

If you get a notice at home telling you to come to the post office to pick up a certified letter, DO SO. If you fail to, by law you are presumed to have received it. You are responsible for its contents. If it is a notice about a hot check, failure to pick up the letter may result in CRIMINAL CHARGES being filed against you. IT NEVER HARMS YOU TO PICK UP THE LETTER. It may harm you greatly if you don't pick it up.

6.17 *Voting Rights.* To register to vote, you must be 18 years old, a U.S. citizen, and a resident in the county in which you wish to vote. You must register 30 days before an election. You can register by mail or in person at the local tax assessor-collector office. College students can choose to vote in their home county or in the county where they attend college.

6.18 *Hazing.* Hazing is a CRIME (see § 2.18 for further information).

6.19 *Rape Prevention.* In a perfect world, you could go anywhere at anytime in perfect safety. However, we must deal with reality. Just as you take precautions to prevent theft and burglary, you should take precautions to prevent rape. Obviously, do not walk down dark streets and alleys alone at night. If you must be out late at night, park in a well-lit area. Get someone to walk you to your car. If alone, approach your car carefully. If the car is locked, have your keys ready before you leave the building. A bunch of keys in your hand with one protruding from a clinched fist makes a good weapon. Always check the inside of the car before getting in, especially if you left the car unlocked.

At home it is safer to keep doors and windows locked, even at night.

SPECIAL NOTE (date or acquaintance rape): Each year, a large number of women are raped by someone they know. While rape is impossible to prevent completely, you can reduce the likelihood by taking some simple steps. Don't invite casual acquaintances back to your home if no one else will be there. If you go to a party alone, don't remain behind while others leave, especially if there has been a lot of drinking. Don't get drunk yourself or remain in the company of a group that is drunk. A group, especially a drunken one, may behave in a manner that no individual member of the group would normally accept. Be careful when flirting. A small segment of the male population believes that every woman is available for sex. They can mistake flirting for a come-on. If they do so, they seldom take "no" for an answer. However, some will accept "no" if you make it clear. This is difficult to do if drinking is involved and if you are alone.

The main defense you have is to be alert to any potential dangers in your situation and eliminate as many of them as possible.

6.20 *What to Do if You Are Raped.* If it happens, in spite of your immediate feelings of pain, embarrassment, humiliation, and anger, there are certain steps you must take in order to prosecute the criminal. The first step is *don't make an immediate decision not to prosecute.* While your feelings of wanting to forget and get on with your life and of wanting to hide what happened are natural, don't make the final decision yet. Take the following steps first. After you've taken them, you can decide later that you don't wish to prosecute, but leave the option open in the beginning.

1. *Do not:* *change clothes; straighten up the scene; shower, bathe, or douche; urinate or defecate.* Any of these steps, while understandable, may destroy valuable evidence to prove you were raped.

2. *Report the rape to:*

a) *Rape crisis center:* If your town has one, it will be listed in the phone book. A trained volunteer will help you with police and doctor. If you do not want to report it to the police, the volunteer will not make you.

b) *Police:* Even if you decide not to prosecute later, it is better to give yourself the option of prosecuting by reporting it to the police as soon as possible. Even a day's delay can mean less evidence available.

3. *Get a medical exam immediately:* Either through your own doctor or the emergency room you must be examined to prove that sexual intercourse took place. Delay makes this more difficult.

4. *Clothes:* Don't change until told to, but be prepared to turn the clothes you were wearing over to the police. Take a change of clothes with you to the medical exam.

5. *Don't suffer alone. Get help!*

6.21 *Should You Prosecute?* An emphatic YES! Most rapists are repeat offenders. If you do not prosecute, he may strike again, either at you or someone else. Even if you feel you don't have enough information about the rapist to prosecute, tell the police everything you know. Your information, however small, may fit in with other information and lead to the capture of the rapist. Tell the police everything you know, even if you don't want to prosecute. Some other victim may wish to do so.

6.22 *If You Are the Party Host Serving Alcoholic Beverages.* In addition to the criminal penalty for providing alcoholic beverages to a minor in § 2.63, you *may,* as a private party host or as an officer or member of an organization that is hosting a party where YOU or YOUR ORGANIZATION provides alcohol, have additional responsibilities. In many states a private party host or officers and members of an organization hosting a party have a legal duty NOT TO SERVE an intoxicated person regardless of age. If an intoxicated person leaves the party and has an accident, the private hosts or officers and members of the organization are legally responsible to pay money for any damages incurred. *Texas* DOES NOT yet have that law. HOWEVER, at least one recent court case has indicated that such a law should exist. It is only smart to protect yourself against a possible lawsuit, by CONTROLLING THE AMOUNT OF ALCOHOL SERVED. Don't let a friend drive home drunk. You may not only be saving his or her life and someone else's, but you may also be saving yourself a lawsuit.

Texas DOES have a law that makes anyone who SELLS ALCOHOLIC BEVERAGES legally responsible if they sell to an intoxicated person and there is an accident.

6.23 *Entering and Traveling in Mexico.* Visiting Mexico can be great fun, but BE CAREFUL. You are subject to all Mexican laws just like a native Mexican. You want to have a good time, not end up a victim of a crime or in jail for breaking the law. PLAY IT SAFE. Stay in groups. Do not go off alone. Moderate your drinking. Good judgment is lost with too much alcohol consumption.

If you are only crossing for a few hours to a border town, Mexican customs does not require you to have a passport or visa. Do have some form of picture identification. If you intend to stay longer, you need a passport, birth certificate, voter's registration card, or affidavit to prove that you are a U.S. citizen. It is best to carry one of those items anyway to avoid any problem in returning to the United States (see § 6.25 below). If you are a permanent resident alien of the United States and wish to stay more than a few hours in Mexico, you must show your U.S. permanent residence card. If you are in the United States on any other visa, contact the nearest Mexican Consulate for visa information. The following cities have consulates:

Austin	(512) 478-2866
Brownsville	(210) 542-4431
Corpus Christi	(512) 882-3375
Dallas	(214) 630-7341
Del Rio	(512) 775-2352
Eagle Pass	(512) 773-9255
El Paso	(915) 533-3644
Houston	(713) 880-8772
Laredo	(512) 723-6369
Midland	(915) 687-2334
San Antonio	(210) 227-9145

SPECIAL NOTE: It is illegal to carry firearms or explosives into Mexico.

6.24 *Driving Your Car in Mexico.* American insurance policies DO NOT cover driving in Mexico. DO NOT drive in Mexico, for even a day, without insurance coverage of some sort, because an ACCIDENT IN MEXICO IS A CRIMINAL OFFENSE. It is likely you will be taken from the scene of the accident directly to the POLICE DEPARTMENT for the amount of DAMAGES to be estimated. If you are judged at fault in the accident, your car is impounded and you can be detained. To be released you must pay cash or have MEXICAN INSURANCE. Therefore, it is best to buy Mexican insurance before you cross the border. The cost is quite reasonable. A policy can be purchased for a single day. For information on Mexican auto insurance, contact an insurance agency that sells Mexican auto coverage. Such agencies are most commonly located in Texas border cities, although you may be able to locate such agencies in all major Texas cities. Listed below are insurance agencies that advertise in the telephone yellow pages that they sell Mexican auto insurance.

BROWNSVILLE
Gallardo's Insurance
(210) 831-3496
Ignacio Martinez Insurance Agency
(210) 542-3079

EAGLE PASS
Hector Barrera Insurance
(210) 773-0927
Sanborn's Mexican Insurance
(210) 773-2341

EL PASO
Aim Insurance Agency
(915) 598-2355
Ruben Enriquez Insurance Agency
(915) 778-4099
Don Green Insurance Agency
(915) 593-4000
El Paso Low Cost Auto Insurance
(915) 757-2277
Gold Key Insurance
(915) 592-7447
Mexican Auto Insurance
(915) 591-7373
Palms Mexico Insurance
(915) 533-0062
Reyna Insurance Agency
(915) 533-0121
Sanborn's Mexican Insurance
(915) 779-3538
Texas Low Cost Insurance Agency
(915) 565-0038 or 778-0186

LAREDO
Camper Center Mexico Insurance Agency
(210) 722-0141
Cavazos Insurance Agency
(210) 723-4623
Johnson's Mexican Insurance
(210) 722-1573
Pena Insurance Agency
(210) 724-9004
Saber Insurance Services, Inc.
(210) 722-1642
Sanborn's Mexican Insurance
(210) 723-3657

MC ALLEN
     Mexican Auto Insurance
          (512) 686-0711
     Mexican Insurance
          (512) 682-3279
     Sanborn's Mexican Auto Insurance
          (512) 686-0711

If you are traveling more than 25 kilometers beyond the Mexican checkpoint, you must carry proof of car ownership with you. A certificate of title or a notarized affidavit of ownership is acceptable to Mexican customs. The Mexican insurance company can help provide the affidavit of ownership. Remember, if you go past the 25 kilometer limit, you also need proof of U.S. citizenship (see § 6.23).

6.25 *Bringing Items Back from Mexico.* If you buy items in Mexico, you should know that certain products CANNOT be brought into the United States and will be confiscated by U.S. Customs *with no reimbursement to you.* PROHIBITED ITEMS include switchblade knives; products made from lizard, snake, crocodile, and sea turtle; ivory; furs of certain species, including jaguar, leopard, tiger, ocelot, margay, tiger cat, seal, and polar bears; most feathers and live birds; many plants, fruits, vegetables, and some meat. Naturally, ILLEGAL DRUGS are also prohibited. You cannot import PETS, lottery tickets, liquor-filled candy, or FIREARMS or AMMUNITION. *You cannot mail alcoholic beverages.*

DUTY FREE ITEMS YOU CAN BRING BACK: One hundred cigars and 200 cigarettes, if *not made in Cuba.* One liter (33.8 fluid ounces) of wine, beer, or liquor can be brought in, *if you are 21 years of age.* You may also bring back $400 worth of goods not on the prohibited list.

REMEMBER, U.S. CUSTOMS DOES NOT HAVE A SENSE OF HUMOR. NO JOKES!

Contact your nearest U.S. Customs office for more information.

6.26 *Returning from Mexico.* To return to the United States you must pass through U.S. Customs. If you are a U.S. citizen, you are not required to have a passport, but you should carry with you some form of photo identification.

SPECIAL NOTE (for noncitizens): If you are a permanent-resident alien be prepared to show your permanent-resident visa.

If you are a nonresident you must present a valid passport with a valid visa. If you are on a student visa, you must show a valid I-20 form showing enrollment in your college or university. Failure to do so may cause REENTRY INTO THE UNITED STATES TO BE DENIED! To enter Mexico, contact the nearest Mexican Consulate for information (see § 6.23 for more information).

Chapter 7
How to Do It Yourself

There are many things you can do to solve problems by yourself. Some are free of charge. This chapter gathers together some of the helpful agencies that are available to you. It also provides some aid in explaining how small claims court works and in hiring a lawyer.

7.1 *Better Business Bureau (BBB).* This is a private, nonprofit agency that helps promote good business practices. Files are kept on BBB members and on any businesses that have had a complaint filed against them. BBB services are free. Use them for two purposes:

1. Check out the business BEFORE you use it. If you're taking your grandmother's wedding dress to be cleaned, check out the cleaners BEFORE you leave the dress. The BBB will have information about any previous unresolved complaints. It doesn't guarantee that you'll be satisfied, of course, but at least you avoid known problems. Do this by phone.

2. AFTER a problem occurs, complain about a problem with a business in writing. The BBB will contact the merchant and attempt to resolve the situation. The BBB works in a spirit of cooperation and cannot compel a business to act. However, most reputable businesses do not want an unresolved complaint report against them at the BBB. That means the business has an incentive to work something out with you.

If the BBB does not resolve the situation to your satisfaction, you can sue in small claims court (see § 7.4).

7.2 *Texas Attorney General's Office for Consumer Affairs (A.G.'s Office).* Branch offices are located in seven Texas cities, whose addresses are listed below.

Make a written complaint to the A.G.'s Office. It can be the same complaint letter you send to the BBB. A letter will be sent to the merchant you have complained about. The A.G.'s Office will attempt to resolve the complaint. If unsuccessful, you still have the right to sue.

The A.G.'s Office specializes in violations of the Texas Deceptive Trade Practices Act, but the A.G.'s Office will accept complaints on other matters.

If enough unresolved complaints are filed with the A.G.'s Office, the A.G. can seek an injunction on behalf of the people of Texas to stop the practice. They have also been successful in reaching out-of-court settlements on problems that affect a large number of consumers.

This service is free. Offices are located in the following cities. If there is not one located in your town or city, file with the closest office.

AUSTIN
P.O. Box 12548
Austin, TX 78711
(512) 463-2070

DALLAS
714 Jackson, Suite 800
Dallas, TX 75202
(214) 742-8944

EL PASO
6090 Surety Dr., Suite 260
El Paso, TX 79905
(915) 772-9476

HOUSTON
1019 Congress, Suite 1550
Houston, TX 77002
(713) 223-5886

LUBBOCK
916 Main Plaza Building,
Suite 806
Lubbock, TX 79401
(806) 747-5238

MC ALLEN
3201 N. McCall Rd.
McAllen, TX 78501
(210) 682-4547

SAN ANTONIO
115 E. Travis
San Antonio, TX 78205
(210) 224-1007

7.3 *Alternative Dispute Resolution Center.* Some cities have available a private, nonprofit, nonjudicial mediation service that attempts to resolve complaints through the use of trained mediators. You file the complaint and the agency sets up a meeting between you, the trained mediator, and the other party. The mediator helps you reach a solution acceptable to all parties.

This system also works on the spirit of cooperation. The agency cannot compel the merchant to participate, but many will. The agency cannot enforce the decision, but mediation frequently works. If it does not, you can still go to court.

Sometimes there is a small charge, and sometimes the service is free. Not all areas have such a service, but more are being created every day. Below are listed those in existence at the time of this writing. If your area is not listed, check with your local police department. The police will usually know if the service exists.

AMARILLO
Dispute Resolution Center
c/o Panhandle Regional Planning Commission
P. O. Box 9257
Amarillo, TX 79105-9257
  (806) 372-3381

AUSTIN
Travis County Dispute Resolution Center
5407 IH 35 N, Suite 410
Austin, TX 78723
  (512) 371-0033

BEAUMONT
Mediation Center of Jefferson County
1149 Pearl, Third Floor, Old Section
Beaumont, TX 77701
  (409) 835-8511

CORPUS CHRISTI
Nueces County Dispute Resolution Center
901 Leopard, Room 110
Corpus Christi, TX 78401
  (512) 888-0650

DALLAS
Dispute Mediation Service of Dallas
3400 Carlisle at Lemmon
Suite 240 LB9
Dallas, TX 75204
  (214) 754-0022

EL PASO
Rio Grande Dispute Resolution Center
1014 N. Stanton, Suite 100
El Paso, TX 79902
  (915) 533-0998

FORT WORTH
    Dispute Resolution Services of Tarrant County, Inc.
    One Summit, Suite 210
    Fort Worth, TX 76102
        (817) 877-4554
HOUSTON
    Dispute Resolution Centers
    Harris County Courthouse Annex
    1302 Preston, Room 100
    Houston, TX 77002
        (713) 755-8274
LUBBOCK
    Regional Center for Dispute Resolution
    1323-58th
    Lubbock, TX 79412
        (806) 762-8721
SAN ANTONIO
    Bexar County Dispute Resolution Center
    300 Dolorosa, Suite 1102
    San Antonio, TX 78205-3009
        (210) 220-2128

7.4 *Small Claims Court.* This is the people's court, set up so that you can use it without hiring a lawyer. Lawyers can be used in small claims court if hired to do so. The judge of the court is the local justice of the peace, and it is located in your county courthouse.

Things are kept simple. The judge's office has a form, called a "petition," that you fill out to file your case. You need the name and *street address* of the party you wish to sue. You must have a street address because the sheriff's office must serve a copy of the petition on the person you are suing. A post office box number won't work. The filing fee can be any amount up to $65. You can request in the petition that the other party has to reimburse you for these court costs, as well as the amount you are suing for.

You can sue for any amount of money up to $5,000. You can only sue for money, not an object, like your TV that your roommate kept. You *can* sue for the value of the TV. Be prepared when you fill out the petition to briefly write the reason why you are suing. By that, I mean be prepared to say that you are suing for your wrongfully withheld $200 property deposit, rather than that you are suing for $200 with no explanation.

You'll be notified about the hearing date. If you need to force witnesses to come to court, you can do so by asking the judge to issue a subpoena. There is an additional charge for this. Ask for the subpoena well in advance of the hearing date, so the sheriff's office will have time to serve the subpoena on your witness.

Before the hearing, the respondent (the party you are suing) may contact you to settle out of court. If the offer is acceptable, take it. If you insist on going to court, there is always the possibility you might lose and get nothing. If you want to recover the filing fee, make that part of your settlement. You do not get the filing fee back from the court if you cancel the case.

Your hearing is really a trial. It will be a trial in front of the judge alone unless you or the respondent asks for a jury trial. There is a small jury fee (about $5). The jury will be made up of six people.

Normally, small claims court trials take place fairly quickly after you file, sometimes in as little as three weeks.

If you decide to hire a lawyer, do so at the beginning of your case or as soon as possible.

If you are representing yourself, make an outline or notes for yourself to help you present your case in a logical and brief fashion.

The judge will give you some help with procedure. Below are some basic rules to follow:

1. In selecting a jury, ask questions of the jury to find out if the jury members are unbiased and have average knowledge of the subject of the suit.

EXAMPLE 1: If you are suing your landlord, find out if any jurors are landlords. Such jurors might tend to side with the landlord. Find out if anyone is, or has ever been, a tenant. That juror might tend to side with you. Those that aren't either one may tend to favor neither side.

EXAMPLE 2: In a traffic accident case, find out if all jurors drive. A nondriver might not be a good juror.

2. You have the right to mark out the names of any three jurors. The respondent has the same right. The first six not struck out will be the jury.

3. If you are the plaintiff, you go first. You may tell your side of the story yourself. You can use notes. When you finish, the respondent gets to ask you questions. That's called "cross-examination."

4. You present all of your side of the case before the respondent presents his or hers.

5. If you have witnesses other than yourself, you must ask them questions like a lawyer would. They cannot just tell their story without questions. The respondent gets to cross-examine them, too.

6. When you are finished with your side of the case, the respondent gets his or her turn. After the respondent testifies, you get to cross-examine the respondent and all of his or her witnesses.

7. After all testimony, the judge or jury makes the decision and announces the winner.

8. Either party can appeal the results to the county court for a new trial if he or she does so within ten days of the judgment. If no appeal occurs within that time period, then the judgment is final.

9. If either party does not show up for the trial, the party that does *show up* wins by default.

10. You must have live witnesses. Sworn written statements are not usually admissible in court. That means you can't use them to help your case.

11. Written estimates of car repair are admissible. It is even better if the estimate is notarized, or you can testify that immediately before the accident, your car was worth $4,000 and immediately after, $3,361.50. Everyone knows that you just subtracted the estimate from the value, but that is one legal way to present the evidence. You can do this even though you are not a mechanic. You can use photographs. It is not required, but it is better to have the person who took the photographs in court to testify about when and where they were taken.

12. If you need to sue for more than $5,000 you must file in a higher court. This means you must hire an attorney.

True Story Number Eighteen

This story has nothing to do with small claims court, but it is too funny to leave out.

Let's visit the Anyones one last time.

Susie Anyone goes to see the attorney for students. She is mad. Her ex-boyfriend has been telling all of their mutual friends terrible things about her. She wants him stopped. She says to the attorney,

"How do I file a suit for DEFECATION of character?" She is extremely puzzled when the attorney bursts out laughing.

If you aren't laughing by this time, go look up "defecation." You undoubtedly would recognize this bodily function by another name.

7.5 *Collecting on a Small Claims Court Judgment.* The trial is the easy part. Getting your money can be the hard part, especially if you are dealing with an individual, like your ex-roommate. It is easier to collect from businesses, but there is no guarantee you'll ever collect. The court DOES NOT help you collect.

Under Texas law, an individual is entitled to have $30,000 worth of personal property (everything but land) *exempt* from being taken to pay a judgment debt. For a married person, the amount is $60,000. There is no garnishment of wages in Texas, except for court-ordered child support. A judgment lien can be placed against land, but the Homestead Act prevents you from forcing a sale of the land if it is a homestead.

The bottom line is that it can be very difficult to collect on a judgment from the average individual. Remember, the personal property exemption of $30,000 covers cars, tools of a trade, furniture, and various personal effects.

Savings accounts, certificates of deposit, stocks and bonds, and goods in excess of $30,000 for a single person or $60,000 for a married person are NOT protected. Any excess in a checking account, over and above reasonable living expenses, can be reached as well. However, a specific legal process must be followed. It takes a lawyer to do this. For the collection of small debts, this is not practical (see [3] below).

Businesses and corporations are usually easier to collect from, especially if they own land.

Since it is so hard to collect, why file in small claims court? Because the debtor you are suing may not *know* how hard it can be to collect from him or her, and therefore, he or she may pay once the judgment is granted. If he or she does not voluntarily pay, you can take the following steps:

1. *Writ of execution:* You pay a hefty fee to the sheriff's office, and a deputy will go out and demand the money. If the person refuses to pay, the deputy CAN DO NOTHING. This is a bluff on your part. Generally, it is a waste of money because the debtor knows the officer can do nothing.

2. *Abstract of judgment:* For a small fee, around $2, you can get a certified copy of the judgment from the justice of the peace court and file it with the county clerk for another small fee ($3). This puts a lien against any land owned by the debtor in THAT COUNTY. If you know of land owned in another county, you can file the certified judgment there too. The lien will attach.

As noted earlier, if the land is a homestead, your lien probably won't do any good because homesteads are protected.

There is one advantage to filing the abstract, even if you know it cannot be attached to any land. Credit-reporting agencies (see § 5.1) usually record any abstract of judgments against the debtor's credit. Wishing to clear up a black mark on credit has caused many debts to be paid.

3. *Hire a lawyer:* This is expensive and therefore not practical for small debts. For a fee, a lawyer will send postjudgment interrogatories. These are questions about what property the debtor owns and where it is. The interrogatories must be answered under oath (before a notary). Failure to do so can result in punishment by the court.

The interrogatories are only worth the cost if the debtor really does own property that is not exempt from seizure. You may or may not know whether this is likely. Remember, you pay for the lawyer's services whether you recover any money on the judgment or not.

7.6 *Finding a Lawyer.* Some situations arise in which you must hire a lawyer for your own best interest, even if you are trying to save money. I have tried to point out some of the situations in this book.

The best way to find a lawyer is to get a referral from a friend who has used the lawyer and been happy with services received. I would take a friend's referral with more caution if your friend merely knows the lawyer as a friend or relative.

Because not everyone will be able to get a referral from a friend, various referral services are available. Participation in referral services by lawyers is voluntary, so not all lawyers are listed. Prices and quality of services are not guaranteed.

The State Bar of Texas has a statewide referral service with a toll-free telephone number, 1-800-932-1900. Tell the operator in what city or county you need a lawyer and for what type of legal problems. You will be given a name.

Some counties and larger cities have local lawyer referral services. Some are listed below. If you do not see one listed for your area, check the yellow pages of the phone book just before the general listing of attorneys. If your area has one, it will be listed there. If it isn't listed, then you don't have a local referral service. These are only some of the referral services available. Check your yellow pages for additional services. These services are free.

ARLINGTON
    Arlington Bar Assn.
    (214) 277-3113
AUSTIN
    Travis County Bar Assn.
    (512) 472-8303
CORPUS CHRISTI
    Nueces County Bar Assn.
    (512) 883-3971
DALLAS
    Dallas Bar Assn.
    (214) 979-9090
    Lawyer Referral Service of Plano
    (214) 424-6113
    Mesquite Bar Assn.
    (214) 270-2102
    North Dallas Bar Assn.
    (214) 980-0472
    Richardson Lawyer Referral Service
    (214) 690-0107
EL PASO
    El Paso Bar Assn.
    (915) 532-7052
FT.WORTH
    Tarrant County Bar Assn.
    (817) 336-4101
HOUSTON
    Harris County Bar Assn.
    (713) 236-8000
    Lawyer Referral Service
    (713) 237-9429
SAN ANTONIO
    Lawyer Referral Service
    (512) 227-1853

Another option is available. At the end of the attorney listings in the yellow pages are separate listings of "board certified in specialties" lawyers. Board certification means the attorney has chosen to take an extra test in his or her special field. Besides passing the test, the lawyer must have been practicing at least five years and must devote a large percentage of his or her practice to that specialty. It does guarantee you that the lawyer has a certain level of expertise in that specialty. However, many good attorneys never choose to take the extra test.

Another option is to read the box advertisements in the yellow pages. These ads usually list the type of cases handled by the lawyer. If a lawyer does only bankruptcy, you don't want to waste time trying to hire him or her for a divorce.

7.7 *Hiring a Lawyer.* I suggest you shop around. Interview several lawyers. Most lawyers do not charge for the first visit unless you hire them. Be sure to ask about a fee when you make the appointment. Compare prices, but more importantly, compare personalities. You want to hire a lawyer that you feel comfortable with, not someone you don't like. On simple cases, like traffic tickets, whether you like the lawyer may not matter. On a more lengthy case, personality matters a great deal.

Don't hesitate to ask questions because you don't want to appear dumb. Lawyers don't expect the nonlawyer to know everything. Sometimes lawyers forget to explain things. ASK.

While it is good to explain your case thoroughly and to ask questions, don't abuse the relationship. The only thing a lawyer has to sell is his or her time and knowledge. Be reasonable in your demands on them.

Understand how you will be charged and for what. Many times you'll be asked to sign a fee contract. Be sure you understand it before you sign.

7.8 *Fees.* There are various ways to charge for legal services. Listed below are the most common ways. The attorney will decide which type of fee is used.

1. ***Flat fee:*** For a set fee of $500 the attorney will represent you. Be sure you understand what's covered. Does it include representing you at trial?

2. ***Hourly fee:*** For so much per hour, say $100, the attorney will represent you. This means that the attorney keeps track of the time used in every phone call, every talk with you or the lawyer for the other side, all time spent in research and in court. The hours can add up. To try to get a realistic idea of the final bill, ask the attorney to estimate the *least* amount of time that a

case like yours would take. Then assume that your case may take more. Amounts per hour vary from lawyer to lawyer and town to town.

3. *Contingent fee:* You pay no fee unless you win the case. You'll be asked to sign a contract stating the percentage of the final judgment or settlement to which the lawyer is entitled. Percentages vary from 25 percent to 40 percent. Under some contracts, if you don't win, you pay expenses, such as court costs. In other contracts you do not have to pay expenses, even if you lose. Contingent fees are most often used in accident cases, malpractice cases, and civil rights cases. This type of fee *cannot* be used in a criminal case.

7.9 *When You Are Not Happy with Your Attorney.* Most attorneys are honest, hardworking, know the law, and do the best possible job for you. Misunderstandings can occur with the best lawyers, and naturally some lawyers are incompetent.

If you are unhappy, set up a face-to-face meeting with your lawyer. If you can't get an appointment, write a letter requesting one, which you send by certified mail, return receipt requested (see § 6.16).

If unable to resolve your dissatisfaction, you have the right to fire the attorney. You can do this yourself or hire a new attorney who will inform your old attorney that he or she is fired. Your old attorney will give your new attorney your file.

You may or may not be entitled to a refund on any money paid to the old attorney. If the old attorney has done some work for you, he or she is entitled to some money, even if you fire the attorney.

If you feel the attorney has acted wrongly, you can file a grievance with the local bar association grievance committee. Find out whom to contact by contacting any attorney or call 1-800-932-1900. This is a free service and can be very effective.

If you have a serious legal malpractice case, you may choose to sue the attorney in court for damages. You must hire an attorney to do this.

7.10 *Free Legal Representation.* Free legal representation is provided in various ways. You usually must meet certain poverty guidelines to be entitled to this free representation.

For criminal matters, either the judge appoints an attorney to represent you, or a public defender office will provide representation (see also § 2.10).

For civil matters, you can get representation several ways. There are various legal aid offices either federally funded or funded through some other agency. To qualify for aid, you must meet the federal poverty guidelines. Because of limited time available, these offices must concentrate on the most serious cases, such as divorce and housing. You may qualify financially, but if you need to probate a will, these offices may not be able to help you. To locate these offices, check under "legal aid" in the phone directory or with the directory assistance operator.

Most communities have lawyers that do occasional work for free. This is called "pro bono" work, from the Latin phrase *pro bono publico.* It means "for the public good." Usually, you are referred to a lawyer for pro bono work by one of the agencies noted above. Sometimes pro bono attorneys have their own referral services listed in the yellow pages of the phone book, just before the general attorney listings. Pro bono work is almost always done through referral only. Don't expect to pick out an attorney's name at random and get him or her to represent you for free.

7.11 *Other Helpful Agencies.*

For discrimination complaints:
Texas Commission on Human Rights
6330 Hwy. 290 East
Ste. 250
Austin, TX 78723
(512) 437-3450

For housing discrimination:
HUD-Fair Housing and Equal Opportunity (FHED)
P.O. Box 2905
Ft. Worth, TX 76113-2905
(817) 885-5521 or Toll Free 1-800-669-9777

Index